D1325131

Wound
Management

theory and practice

Mick Miller   RGN, DPSN, BSc (Hons)

Deborah Glover   RGN, BSc (Joint Hons), PGDip

Acknowledgements

The editors would like to thank all the authors who kindly contributed to this book, many of whom were asked to write chapters at fairly short notice. We would also like to thank NT Publishing for agreeing to produce the book and all the staff there who have worked hard to turn the edited text and pictures into the final production.

The contents of this publication are the views of the individual authors and do not necessarily represent the views of Johnson & Johnson Medical Ltd.

First published 1999 by Nursing Times Books
Emap Healthcare Ltd, part of Emap Business Communications
Greater London House
Hampstead Road
London NW1 7EJ

Text © 1999 Emap Healthcare Ltd

Cover image: *Pseudomonas aerugninosa:* Dr Linda Stannard/Science Photo Library.

Printed and bound in Great Britain by The Friary Press, Dorchester, Dorset.

British Library cataloguing in Publication Data
A catalogue record for this book is available from the British Library.

ISBN: 1 902499 11 5

Contents

Introduction

Why produce another book about wound management? That was one of the questions that we asked ourselves when embarking on this project. The answer? Well, quite simply, because there is still a huge demand for information about this topic that does not seem to be satisfied by the articles and books published to date. Commissioning and editing this book also provided an opportunity to ask experts in the field to put their latest ideas and experience into print. As one works within a specialist area of practice, tactics of communicating concepts develop and improve. This publication has given specialists the chance to publish their up-to-date conceptual thinking.

We also wanted to produce a text that was accessible and easy to read, one that provided the basic information needed for the average nurse, if there is such a person, to acquire an introduction to the theory of all aspects of wound management. To this end we briefed the authors to 'keep it straightforward'. We wanted good-quality information but for it to be presented using uncomplicated and easily understood language. More extensive discussion, however, has been included in the chapter on growth factors as this is a relatively new area which many believe will play a significant role in the future of wound therapy.

We have gone to great lengths to include as many colour plates in the text as possible, because seeing is often more useful than reading. The editors have also included a list of main issues at the beginning of each chapter to enable the reader to get a good idea of chapter contents before reading the text.

We hope that the book will encourage nurses to develop a greater understanding of an area that can seem mystifying and complex but is, perhaps, more straightforward than many people think.

Mick Miller
Deborah Glover
July 1999

The editors

Mick Miller, RGN, DPSN, BSc (Hons)

Mick Miller started to specialise in wound management while working in accident and emergency. He wrote protocols for wound care in A&E, set up a nurse-run dressing clinic and began to lecture and write about various aspects of tissue viability.

In 1993 he joined the Tissue Repair Research Unit (TRRU), Guy's Hospital, London, as Clinical Nurse Specialist. While there he was involved in setting up and running a specialist wound clinic, managing clinical trials and providing clinical consultancy and education related to wound management and tissue viability. He became Assistant Director of Clinical Research at the unit in 1995.

He has written regularly for a variety of nursing journals and has lectured on wound management and related issues at over 200 venues in the UK over the past five years.

He is now Clinical Education Manager for the Johnson & Johnson Medical Wound Management Business Unit, responsible for designing and instigating educational initiatives such as books, videos, CD ROMs and conferences, for nurses throughout the UK. He a also a committee member of the Wound Care Society.

Deborah Glover, RGN, BSc (Joint Hons), PGDip

Deborah Glover qualified as an RGN in 1983 after training at University College Hospital, London. She has worked in several clinical areas including care of the elderly, oncology, ITU, and HIV. Prior to becoming clinical editor at Nursing Times, she undertook several practice and professional development roles, many of which involved working with clinical staff in the formulation and implementation of pressure sore prevention and management policies and wound care guidelines. As part of her role as clinical editor, she manages the wound care supplement.

Contributors

Andrea Andrews, BSc
Manager, Biosurgical Research Unit
Surgical Materials Testing Laboratory

Kate Ballard, RGN, BSc (Hons)
Research Nurse, Tissue Repair Research Unit
Guys Hospital

Mark Collier, BA (Hons), RGN, ONC, RCNT, RNT
Nurse Consultant/Senior Lecturer (Tissue Viability)
Thames Valley University

Pam Cooper, RN, DPSN
Clinical Nurse Specialist, Department of Tissue Viability
Aberdeen Royal Infirmary

Keith Cutting, MN, RMN, RGN, Dip N (Lond), Cert Ed (FE)
Principal Lecturer
Buckinghamshire Chilterns University College

Madeleine Flanagan, MA, BSc, DipN, Cert Ed, ONC, RGN
Principle Lecturer, Tissue Viability
University of Hertfordshire

Ali Foster, BA (Hons), PGCE, DPodM, MShS, SCRh
Chief Podiatrist
King's College Hospital

Ann Fowler, RGN, DPSN
Clinical Nurse Specialist, Burns
Mount Vernon & Watford Hospitals NHS Trust

Marsh Gelbart, BA, MA, RGN, HV
Freelance Journalist and Health Advisor Chelsea & Westminster Hospital, London

Brian Gilchrist, BSc, MSc, RGN
Lecturer
King's College

David Gray, RN
Clinical Nurse Specialist, Department of Tissue Viability
Aberdeen Royal Infirmary

Sylvie Hampton, BSc (Hons), DPSN, RGN
Tissue Viability Nurse Specialist
Eastbourne Hospital

Dr Jeff Hart, PhD
Wound Repair Research Group
St. James's University Hospital

Mary Jones, BN, RGN, DN
Senior Clinical Research Nurse
Surgical Materials Testing Laboratory

Mick Miller, RGN, DPSN, BSc (Hons)
Clinical Education Manager
Johnson & Johnson Medical, Wound Management Business Unit

Robert John Moorehead, MD, FRCS
Consultant surgeon
The Ulster Hospital

Captain Sally Simmons, RGN, CHRN (US), Dip Asthma Management, RCGP/NATC
Deputy Head, Health Care Assistant Training
Royal Defence Medical College

Michael CR Whiteside, MD, FRCS
Senior Registrar
The Ulster Hospital Belfast

Dr Stephen Young, PhD
Director, Tissue Viability Unit
Guys Hospital

1 Wounds in time: the history of wound management

Marsh Gelbart

Key points

- Historical documentation of wound treatment dates back 2000 years BC
- Materials used to cover wounds through the ages have included mud, meat and grease
- As early as the fifth century BC, Hippocrates documented the importance of cleanliness in wound care
- Injuries have become more complex through history owing to the involvement of mechanical devices
- The doctrine of laudable pus played an important role in early wound therapies
- The germ theory was responsible for important changes in wound management
- Some ancient remedies, such as honey and sugar, are again being used today

The human body has always been subject to injury and throughout history efforts have been made to repair the damage. In earliest times, injuries were typically caused by conflict with other people, accidents or animals. The nature of the damage was comparatively simple, involving lacerations, fractures and crush injuries. More recently, injuries have become more complex as mechanical devices have superseded animals as a major cause of trauma and weapons of war have become increasingly destructive.

A number of common threads connect wound care through the ages. First, some procedures can do more harm than good. Second, the occasional rediscovery of ancient techniques and their adoption for current use. Third, warfare, despite the suffering it brings, has accelerated advances in wound care.

In addition, medical opinion in successive civilisations was contradictory. It veered between identifying wound sepsis as a problem to be avoided or as a commendable sign of wound healing. These misunderstandings had obvious consequences for wound care.

Wound care BC

Mud and leaves were among the first materials used to cover wounds and encourage haemostasis. Acacia thorns and their attached vegetable fibres were probably used to suture wounds, a technique still used by some indigenous people in southern Africa (Knight, 1981). In Babylon, around 2250 BC, sesame oil was applied to wounds to inhibit the growth of staphylococci (Majno, 1991).

Translations of medical papyri from the second millennium BC reveal that the Egyptians were capable of minor surgery on wounds, abscesses and easily accessible tumours (McGrew, 1983). Sutures of linen were used for wound closure (Hauben, 1985). Some of the dressings applied to wounds, such as meat, were probably of little practical use. Others, such as honey, were possibly more beneficial, as the osmotic activity caused by honey and sugar pastes helps break down bacteria (Topham, 1996).

In the fifth century BC, rhinoplasties were performed in India. Sutures made of hair were used to close the wounds and leaves and oils were used as dressings (Whipple, 1963a). These surgical techniques were more advanced than those practised in Europe. Indian practitioners understood that some external factor was involved in the formation of sepsis, so sick rooms were fumigated (Mukhopadhyaya, 1973).

Classical Greece influenced many of the West's medical traditions. For example, Hippocrates (460–370 BC) emphasised caution and cleanliness in wound care (Hauben, 1985). Clean wounds were left undressed, but others were washed and covered in clean linen soaked in wine or vinegar. Inflamed wounds were irrigated with sea water, as it had been noted that fishermen's wounds seldom suppurated. They were then left to heal by first intention.

Other Greek physicians believed in bleeding and purging a patient to avoid wound inflammation. If a wound's edge was ragged and badly contused, then in these cases Hippocrates agreed that suppuration should be encouraged. It was seen as part of the healing process (Hauben, 1985). Although much of the thrust of Hippocrates' thought was that wounds, where possible, should heal by first intention, in the years to come, many healers would disregard this. There grew up in Greek and Roman medicine a doctrine of laudable pus, whereby doctors were encouraged to seek suppuration in all wounds that came to their attention. This misinterpretation would have an enormous impact on wound care in the centuries to follow (Knight, 1981).

Wound care AD

By the first century AD, Roman armies had an efficient network of military hospitals. A common medicament was made by dissolving myrrh resin into water. The resultant solution was bacteriostatic acting against *Staphylococcus aureus* and other Gram-positive bacteria (Majno, 1991).

Celsus (25 BC–50 AD) believed that the main priorities in wound care were to stop haemorrhaging and avoid inflammation. Vinegar-soaked sponges were used to stanch bleeding and, if this approach failed, then vessels were tied or cauterised with a hot blade. The wounds were cleaned with vinegar and the edges brought together with woollen sutures. If wounds over-granulated when healing, then a paste containing rust flakes and verdigris was applied (Cope, 1958).

Galen (129–199 AD), the most venerated medical authority in the empire, noted that wounds healed when irrigated with wine and sutured. However, he also advocated the concept of laudable pus.

Struggling against dogma

The doctrine of laudable pus exerted a malignant grip on medicine and individual physicians had to struggle towards a better understanding of the healing process.

Between 1205 and 1320 Theodoric and de Mondeville refuted the laudable pus concept and promoted primary (or first intention) wound healing. They believed that wounds should simply be cleaned and debrided, the sides wiped dry with lint soaked in wine and the edges sutured and bandaged. Even though in the 12th and 13th centuries Italian medical schools advocated less caustic wound treatments, the acceleration of suppuration was still supported by many.

Between 1300 and 1368 Guy de Chauliac dressed and packed wounds, first with egg whites then astringents. They were repeatedly reopened until pus formed. Dressings usually consisted of readily available materials such as cotton, flannel or wool. These would be soaked in ointment, inserted into the wound and used to cover the injury. Dressings were frequently reused as there was no understanding of asepsis.

Lay people also used their own remedies. It is known that English archers at the battlefield of Crécy in 1346 collected spider webs to lay across their wounds in order to arrest bleeding. Not all medieval medicine was erroneous, however. An English manuscript dated 1446 shows that recommended treatment regimes were sometimes 'systemic and rational' (Kirpatrick and Naylor, 1997). Some wounds were probed with a parsley stick to gauge depth and involvement of other organs. Caustic substances such as ferrous sulphate were used to expose and debride wounds which were then cleaned with milder desloughing agents and astringents.

Finally granulation was encouraged by a dressing containing resins and soothing volatile substances such as rose oil. For deep ulcers, a dressing pack known as a tent was made up of the pith of a plant such as elderflower. Pith had the advantage of being light, absorbent and easily obtainable.

The Aztecs

In South America, where the doctrine of laudable pus was never established, some wound treatment regimes were quite sophisticated. Healers of the warlike Aztec empire had plenty of chance to practise their arts. If a bone fracture failed to unite, a branch of fir wood was inserted in the marrow. This technique, known as marrow pegging, was not rediscovered until the battlefields of the early 20th century.

Wound care was equally sophisticated, with wounds encouraged to heal by primary intention. They were irrigated with fresh urine and Matlaxihuitl, a herb with haemostatic properties, was applied to stem bleeding. Finally the concentrated sap of the maguey plant was mixed with salt and placed on the wound. This had strong anti-bacterial and fungicidal effects (Davidson and Ortez De Montellano, 1983).

Gunpowder poison

The arrival of gunpowder on the battlefield complicated wound management. Lead balls from primitive firearms smashed bone, tore vessels and drove particles of clothing into victim's bodies. Gross contamination of the wound was frequent. Sepsis was inevitable.

In an era when understanding of bacteriology was poor, the consequences were devastating. Almost all surgery of the period was performed on war injuries. Many of those wounded by firearms died. Not surprisingly, it was believed that gunpowder itself was poisonous.

In an attempt to arrest bleeding in gunshot wounds and to nullify the 'gunpowder poison', the standard treatment was cautery. Cauterisation was performed by applying red-hot blades or by pouring boiling oil into wounds. Many common soldiers preferred other approaches such as a 'magical' salve. This was made from ingredients such as human remains and earthworms. The salve was then applied to their own weapons in the belief that it would protect them from injury and the surgeon's attentions (Whipple, 1963a).

Paré (1510 – 1590), a French military surgeon, believed in the effectiveness of cautery by heated oil. However, in 1537 during the siege of Naples, he ran out of oil. In desperation he applied a salve of eggs, rose oil and turpentine to gunshot wounds. To his surprise, the outcome of the new treatment was an improvement (Porter, 1963).

Wound care remained static for much of the next two-and-a-half centuries despite advances in anatomy and physiology.

Era	Treatment	Purpose	Where used
2250 BC	Sesame oil	Counteract *Staphylococcus aureus*	Babylon
2000 BC	Honey and sugar	Osmosis aids breakdown of bacteria	Egypt
500 BC	Hair	Suturing wounds	India
460–370 BC	Sea water	Wound irrigation	Greece
100 AD	Myrrh resin Vinegar-soaked sponge Cautery Rust flakes and verdigris	Bacteriostatic Stanch bleeding Prevent over-granulation	Roman armies
150 AD	Irrigation with wine	Wound cleansing	Roman Empire

1200 – 1400	Egg white and oil of roses;
	  spider webs
		Packed into wound
		  to stop bleeding
			Europe

1400	Ferrous sulphate Parsley sticks Resins and rose oil 'Tent' of elderflower pith	Wound debridement To gauge wound depth To encourage granulation To pack wounds	Europe
1300 – 1519	Fir wood into bone Urine and Matlalxihuitl herb Maguey sap	Internal fixation Wound cleansing Stem bleeding; antibacterial	South America
1500	Hot oil/blades Human remains and earthworms	Cautery 'Magical' salve	Europe
	Eggs, turpentine and rose oil	Salve	Europe
1793	Adhesive plaster strips	Primary closure	Europe

Table 1 Treatments through the ages; early times to the end of the 18th century

Self-repair

Hunter (1728–1793) believed that the human body could be considered a machine with powers of self-repair. He saw the job of the surgeon as being to facilitate this self-repair by helping to close wounds. He was an advocate of healing by first intention. Bandaging, interrupted threaded sutures and adhesive strips were all used by Hunter's contemporaries to close incisions (Cope, 1958).

Noting the sepsis that often appeared around the puncture wounds formed by sutures, Hunter preferred adhesive plaster strips for wound closure. His genius was constrained by two factors, the pain barrier and wound sepsis.

Anaesthesia

Nitrous oxide was discovered by Priestley in 1772. Davey noted its analgesic effect in 1798 and suggested its use in operations. Its was first used in 1842 for a tooth extraction. Advances in anaesthesia followed rapidly. In 1846 ether was used by Morton in Boston, while chloroform was utilised a year later in Edinburgh by Simpson. A new era in medicine had been ushered in (Whipple, 1963b).

The introduction of anaesthesia allowed surgeons to attempt longer and more complicated procedures. However, without an understanding of bacteriology, post-operative mortality rates continued to be high. The pain barrier had been broken, but the problem of sepsis remained (Whipple, 1963b).

Bacteria and weapons

Wound care from the 1860s to the early 1900s was marked by two key processes, one positive, the other counter-productive. The first was the growth in understanding of the role of bacteria in wound sepsis, with resulting improvements in wound care. The second involved advances in military technology. The injuries caused by new weapons were appalling and casualties were inflicted on an unprecedented scale. In many ways the increasing capacity of soldiers to inflict harm outstripped the ability of surgeons to repair it.

Beating bacteria

Anaesthesia had allowed surgeons to carry out an increased range of challenging operations. Patients did not die as frequently on the operating table from shock and pain, but death rates remained high owing to infection. The next great advance in wound care was the concept of asepsis.

Joseph Lister (1827–1912) became Professor of Surgery in Glasgow in 1860. He puzzled over certain facts. A patient with a closed fracture was likely to recover, no matter how severe the injury, but a patient with even the simplest compound fracture was likely to lose life or limb.

Lister postulated that some aspect of air itself was responsible for sepsis. His ideas were confirmed on learning of Pasteur's work on the causes of putrefaction. The Dutch draper Antoni van Leeuwenhoek (1632–1723) had first discovered the existence of tiny micro-organisms. He had found these in scrapings from his own dental plaque. Pasteur's research had confirmed that similar microbes were responsible for fermentation and putrefaction and that the cause of various diseases could be traced to specific organisms. Pasteur also demonstrated that microbes could be destroyed by heat. The question facing Lister was how to prevent bacteria being present within an operating theatre and entering a wound (Porter, 1997)?

Lister adopted the use of carbolic acid as an antiseptic. This had proved effective in cleansing the stinking sewers of Carlisle. He used carbolic mist sprays to suppress the bacterial contamination of operating theatres. He also used carbolic to disinfect cat-gut sutures. Mortality rates after amputations on Lister's wards dropped from 46% to 15% (Porter, 1997).

In August 1865 a young boy, James Greenlees, was successfully operated on for a compound fracture of his left leg. Carbolic acid was mixed with water in the ratio of 1:20 and used to soak his wound dressings. Lister's wound dressing was sophisticated for its day. It consisted of an eightfold layer of gauze, with a strip of Mackintosh between the seventh and eighth layer. The waterproof Mackintosh helped prevent microbes in the air from getting to the wound. A layer of silk was placed between the wound itself and the gauze to protect it from the carbolic acid (Laffin, 1970).

Lister later realised that microbes found on the skin and clothing of theatre staff were more of a hazard than micro-organisms in the air. He abandoned the use of his carbolic mist sprays but encouraged the washing of surgeons' hands and instruments in carbolic solution.

Lister's techniques were of enormous benefit in preventing infection but did little to heal wounds that were already infected and suppurating. He did not believe that his antiseptics could sterilise wounds which already had an established infection, although many other surgeons did (Cope, 1958).

Aseptic procedures used in operating theatres gradually evolved into those recognised today. In Berlin, in 1886, the steam sterilisation of metal surgical instruments was introduced by von Bergmann. In 1890 Halsted introduced sterilised rubber gloves to the operating theatres of Baltimore. In 1900 Hunter introduced gauze masks for operating theatre staff at Charing Cross Hospital (Whipple, 1963a).

Killing tools

The greatest challenge in trauma care was coping with war-related injuries. The nature of wounds caused by firearms is very specific. When a high-velocity bullet hits a body, it transfers its energy to tissue at the point of impact. As the bullet penetrates, a shock wave is transmitted into flesh, muscle tissue and internal organs. For a few microseconds the shock causes a temporary cavity to appear. This cavity, some 30 times the diameter of the bullet, surrounds the bullet's track. As the cavity collapses, it sucks in surface debris, scraps of clothing and skin flora (Owen-Smith, 1982).

Soldiers in the field have little chance to wash or change clothes. Their skin tends to be colonised by *Escherichia coli* which slowly spreads from tiny pieces of faecal matter around the anus. As these harmful bacteria are sucked deep into the wound, tissue becomes grossly contaminated (McManners, 1994).

War wounds were also caused by fragments from exploding artillery shells. These are generally of lower velocity than bullets, but their killing effect is augmented by the blast and pressure waves experienced at the site of an explosion.

New techniques were introduced in an attempt to care for the wounded. Blood transfusions were introduced in the Franco-Prussian war of 1870 which also saw the introduction of primary field dressings. These consisted of pre-prepared packages of sterile lint in a waterproof wrapping which soldiers could apply to wounds as first aid.

The 1905 Russo-Japanese war saw a combination of new techniques for wound care and a fallback to folk remedies. As an example of cutting-edge medical technology, Japanese surgeons used nickel-plated steel pins to peg together shattered long bones. Yet at the same hospital in Osaka shortages of conventional dressings meant that a bird-lime salve had to be used to dress wounds (Macpherson, 1908).

The abattoir

The First World War of 1914–1918 was the largest man-made slaughterhouse in human history. Amidst all the suffering, however, new methods of dressing and treating wounds came to light.

The mud and filth found in trench warfare meant that tetanus infected nine of every 1,000 wounds (Porter, 1997). Mortality among those affected by tetanus was high, running at 78%. However, anti-toxins introduced by Sir David Bruce meant that the mortality rate dropped to 15% by 1919 (Laffin, 1970).

Injuries produced by high-velocity projectiles tended to be infected by soil and other contaminants. *Colstridium welchii*, an anaerobic spore-bearing bacterium found in soil, often found its way into penetrative wounds. The result was gas gangrene (Hollinworth, 1993).

The first stage of battlefield wound care was to stop haemorrhage and stabilise the patient. Once that had been done the casualty was transferred to a base hospital within 12 hours. There, wounds were vigorously debrided. The surface area of soft tissue wounds was enlarged and visible contaminants cut away. Tissue destroyed by cavitation also needed to be excised. This initially appeared undamaged and required an experienced surgeon accurately to gauge the amount of necrosis.

Wounds needed to be left open or perhaps lightly packed with gauze, in order to give tissue a chance to recover before being sutured. This usually took place five days after debridement. It was known as delayed primary closure and is still effective today.

Initially hypertonic salt solutions and flavine compounds were used to irrigate wounds. British field hospitals also used BIPP paste. This consisted of bismuth nitrate, iodine and liquid paraffin (Morison, 1918). By the end of the war Dakin's solution (a hypochlorite preparation) was favoured for irrigation (Cope, 1958) and gauze, sometimes impregnated with paraffin as *tulle gras*, was used to pack wounds loosely.

The First World War saw other advances in surgery and trauma care. Abdominal, chest and head wounds, which would previously have resulted in mortality, were operated on successfully. Harold Gillies and others pioneered plastic surgery for facial wounds by using pedicle skin grafts. The importance of early splinting and stabilisation of fractures was reinforced (Porter, 1997).

Era	Treatment	Purpose	Where used
1865	Carbolic acid	Disinfection of operating theatres. Also used to soak wound dressings	Scotland
1870	Pre-packaged, sterile wound dressings	Prevention of bleeding and protect wounds	Franco/Prussian war
1886	Steam sterilisation of metal surgical instruments	Antibacterial	Germany
1890	Sterilised rubber gloves	Protection of patient from skin flora carried by surgeons	America
1905	Nickel-plated steel pegs	Fixation of complex fractures	Japan
1905	Bird lime	Wound dressing	Japan
1914–1918	Debridement and delayed closure of contaminated wounds	Prevention of infection and improvement of healing	The Great War
1914–1918	Paraffin gauze (*tulle gras*)	Wound dressing	The Great War
1914–1918	Hypochlorite solutions	Debriding and dressing of wounds	The Great War
1914-1918	Pedicle grafts	Treatment of burns	The Great War
1919	Development of tetanus anti-toxin	Treatment of tetanus	The Great War

Table 2 Treatments through the ages. 1800s – 1919

Maggots

During the Great War it was noted that wounds infested by maggots healed well because maggots removed necrotic tissue. In the 1930s, Stanton Livingston, an American orthopaedic surgeon, built upon this knowledge. He treated problematical surgical wounds with specially bred sterile greenbottle maggots (Garner, 1997). Livingston used the larvae on compound comminuted fractures. The wound site was packed with gauze for 48 hours to control haemorrhage, then irrigated with saline. The maggots were then inserted. The dressing and the maggots were renewed every five days. Livingston believed that there was an interaction between the maggots and the exudate in a wound which produced a bacteriophage. This was able to destroy certain bacteria, particularly streptococci and staphylococci.

Many of the wounded survivors of the Great War were affected by the torment of osteomyelitis. Livingston extracted the active bacteriophage from the bodies of maggots ground up in saline and applied the solution to infected bone (Garner, 1997). Results were claimed to be better than those obtained by other methods used at the time. These included the application of Vaseline packs and attempts to sterilise the wound site chemically through topical applications. Once antibiotics were introduced, maggot therapy fell out of favour. Recently, however, it has started to be used again (Jones and Champion, 1998).

Antibiotics – sepsis and serendipity

The discovery of penicillin and sulphonamide revolutionised wound care and the fight against sepsis. Penicillin was discovered in 1929 at St Mary's Hospital, London. A petri dish containing a staphylococcus culture had become contaminated by a mould. Dr Alexander Fleming noted that the mould destroyed the staphylococcus. He soon discovered that the mould, which he named penicillin, would also kill pneumococci and streptococci while not harming animal tissue. Fleming was unable to extract pure penicillin from his experimental broths. However, his work was further developed by Florey and Chain.

Penicillin was first used in February 1941. The patient was a policeman who had nicked himself shaving and was dying of a staphylococcal infection. Although the infection responded to penicillin, there were insufficient quantities of the drug to continue treatment, despite small amounts of penicillin being filtered from the patient's urine and reused after purification. When the penicillin ran out, the patient died. A similar process occurred with the next patient. On the third attempt the small stock of available penicillin proved adequate. A fifteen-year-old boy survived a surgical wound infection which, without the intervention of an antibiotic, would have proved lethal (Reidman and Gustafson, 1995).

Penicillin had been preceded by another useful tool in the fight against wound infection – sulphonamide. In the 1930s Leonard Colebrook had been investigating *haemolytic streptococcus* in childbirth and discovered antibacterial properties in a dye, Prontosil (Bale and Jones, 1997). By 1935 it had been established that sulphonamide was the active ingredient of Prontosil. Sulphonamide proved effective against streptococcal infections. The drug could be given systematically or applied locally, sprinkled directly on to the raw tissues of a traumatic injury. Sulphonamides, although useful, were eclipsed once penicillin became readily available (Bale and Jones, 1997).

War as catalyst

The conflicts of the 1930s accelerated developments in wound care. Trueta, a surgeon working during the Spanish Civil War, demonstrated that septic wounds would recover if completely immobilised in plaster of Paris (Cope, 1958). This method had been adopted in desperation as a result of a lack of alternate dressings or treatments.

During the Second World War casualty survival rates demonstrated a marked improvement when compared to those of the First World War. This occurred partly as a consequence of advances in surgical techniques but mainly owing to the widespread availability of blood transfusions and antibiotics.

The introduction of reconstructive surgery for burn patients heralded a new era in treatment. Up until 1940 the application of tannic acid or gentian violet was common. These solidified into a film over the burns. The intention was to reduce pain, but the result was increased infection. Archibald McIndoe replaced tannic acid and gentian violet with immersion in salt water baths. He also pioneered plastic surgery for those who had suffered the appalling burns caused by high-octane aviation fuel. Some current techniques used in the treatment of burns are still based on McIndoe's work (Gelb, 1986).

Modern practice

In the last decade the suitability of several of the traditional solutions used for wound care have been reassessed. Hypochlorites such as Eusol, which are thought by some to damage new vessels and cells in healing wounds, have fallen out of favour (Leaper and Simpson, 1986).

Recently there has been a profound change in the nature of wound dressings. Technologically sophisticated materials are now available. Up until the 1960s a clean, dry wound was the optimum aim. A series of experiments by George Winter (1962) and other researchers (Hinman and Maibach, 1963; Dyson et al, 1988) began to change prevailing opinion about wound dressings. It was established that wounds protected by an occlusive dressing that created a moist environment at the wound bed healed faster than those left to dry out. Since then, dressings have been developed which are non-adherent, able to debride, maintain a warm environment and manage wound exudate.

Era	Treatment	Purpose	Where used
1930s	Maggots	Removing dead tissue, particularly in the treatment of osteomyelitis	America
1935	Sulphonamide as a topical or systemic agent	Anti-bacterial effect	Germany
1936-1938	Plaster of Paris	Used to immobilise limbs and cover infected wounds	Spain
1940	Plastic surgery for burns	Functional restoration	England
1941	Penicillin, as a topical or systemic agent	Antibiotic	England
1970s	Modern occlusive dressings	Wound coverings	Widely used

Table 3 Treatments through the ages; 1930s to current era

Conclusion

Wound management has a varied history of development. From ancient cultures with a primitive understanding of the mechanisms of healing to those with a more scientific approach, the process has been both haphazard and innovative. Wound management continues to evolve today with the introduction of new technologies such as wound stimulants containing growth factors. Alongside this some more traditional therapies, such as the use of maggots, are being revisited. It is inevitable that wound management will continue to be a dynamic and developing field in the future.

References

Bale, S., Jones,V. (1997) *Wound Care Nursing: A Patient-Centred Approach*. London: Baillière Tindall.

Cope, Z. (1958) The treatment of wounds through the ages. *Medical History;* 2: 163–174.

Davidson, J., Ortez De Montellano, B. (1983) The antibacterial properties of an Aztec wound remedy. *Journal of Ethnopharmacology;* 8: 149–161.

Dyson, M. et al (1988) Comparison of the effects of moist and dry conditions on dermal repair. *Journal of Investigative Dermatology;* 91: 5, 435–439.

Garner, L. (1997) S.K. Livingston and the maggot therapy of wounds. *Military Medicine;* 162: 296–300.

Gelb, N. (1986) *Scramble: A Narrative History of the Battle of Britain. London*: Pan.

Hauben, D. (1985) The Evolution of wound healing by first intention: (a short history of wound treatment). *Koroth;* 8: 11–12, 77–88.

Hinman, C. D., Maibach, H. (1963) Effects of air exposure and occlusion on experimental human skin wounds. *Nature;* 200: 377–378.

Hollinworth, H. (1993) Managing a patient with an infected foot ulcer. *Journal of Wound Care;* 2: 1: 22–26.

Jones, M., Champion, A. (1998) Nature's way. *Nursing Times;* 94: 34, 75–78.

Kirpatrick, J.J.R., Naylor, I.L. (1997) Ulcer management in medieval England. *Journal of Wound Care;* 6: 7, 350–352.

Knight, B. (1981). The history of wound care. Wound Care Supplement No. 2. *Nursing Times* 77; 43, 5–8.

Laffin, J. (1970). *Surgeons in the Field*. London: J.M. Dent and Sons.

Leaper, D.J., Simpson, R.A. (1986) The effect of antiseptics and topical antimicrobials on wound healing. *Journal of Antimicrobial Chemotherapy;* 17: 2, 135–137.

Macpherson, W.G. (1908) *The Russo-Japanese War; Medical and Sanitary Reports from Officers Attached to the Japanese and Russian Forces in the Field*. London: War Office.

Majno, G. (1991) *The Healing Hand: Man and Wound in the Ancient World*. Cambridge Massachusetts: Harvard University Press.

McGrew, R. (1983) *Encyclopedia of Medical History*. London: Macmillan Press.

McManners, H. (1994) *The Scars of War*. London: Harper Collins.

Morison, R. (1918). *BIPP Treatment of War Wounds*. London: Oxford University Press.

Mukhopadhyaya, G. (1973) *The Surgical Instruments of the Hindus*. New Delhi: P.K. Naahar and Co.

Owen-Smith, M. (1982) The traumatic wounds of warfare. Wound Care Supplement No. 13. *Nursing Times;* 78: 38, 49–52.

Porter, R., (ed.) (1963). *Medicine: A History of Healing; Ancient Traditions to Modern Practices.* London: Michael O'Mara Books.

Reidman, S., Gustafson E. (1995). Green mould in the wind. In: Carey, J. (ed.) *The Faber Book of Science.* London: Faber and Faber.

Topham, J. (1996) Sugar paste and povidone-iodine in the treatment of wounds. *Journal of Wound Care;* 5: 8, 364–365.

Whipple, A. (1963a) *The Story of Wound Healing and Wound Repair.* Springfield, Illinois: Charles C. Thomas.

Whipple, A. (1963b) *The Evolution of Surgery in the United States.* Springfield, Illinois: Charles C. Thomas.

Winter, G. (1962) Formulation of the scab and the rate of epithelialisation in the skin of the domestic pig. *Nature;* 193: 293–294.

2 The physiology of wound healing

Madeleine Flanagan

Key points

▶ The physiology of wound healing is a fragile and complex process that is dependent on many inter-related factors

▶ A basic understanding of the body's physiological response to injury is necessary if practitioners are to plan appropriate wound management and to evaluate the effectiveness of treatment

▶ Careful assessment can help to identify the different phases of healing, which is important as treatment objectives may vary during each stage

▶ Inappropriate wound management can occur when practitioners fail to differentiate between healthy and abnormal healing characteristics

▶ To avoid ambiguity when describing wounds it is important to use appropriate terminology and to ensure that colleagues understand the terms used

Introduction

Wound healing is a complex physiological process that is dependent on a number of inter-related factors. Wound assessment and treatment should be based on an understanding of normal tissue repair and factors affecting the process. This chapter describes the stages of wound healing, with the implications that each has for clinical practice.

The process of wound healing

All tissues in the body are capable of healing by one of two mechanisms: regeneration or repair. Regeneration is the replacement of damaged tissues by identical cells and is more limited than repair. In humans, complete regeneration occurs in a limited number of cells, for example, epithelial, liver and nerve cells. The main healing mechanism is repair, where damaged tissue is replaced by connective tissue which then forms a scar. Wound healing can be defined as the physiology by which the body replaces and restores function to damaged tissues (Tortora and Grabowski, 1996).

Local conditions for optimal wound healing

The provision of a supportive micro-environment at the wound surface is of the utmost importance when trying to maximise a wound's healing potential (Winter and Scales, 1963). Maintaining a controlled set of local conditions that is able to sustain the complex cellular activity occurring in wound healing should be the primary aim of wound management.

In simple terms the process of wound healing can be divided into four dynamic phases:

▶ vascular response

▶ inflammatory response

▶ proliferation

▶ maturation

There is considerable overlap between these phases, and the time needed by an individual to progress to the next phase of healing depends on a multitude of factors. These are documented in detail elsewhere (Krasnor, 1996; Flanagan, 1997).

Careful assessment should help to identify each stage of wound healing. This is important as treatment objectives may differ as each phase of healing progresses. Inappropriate wound management often occurs owing to the practitioner's inability to differentiate between normal and abnormal characteristics associated with wound healing (Bennett and Moody, 1995).

The vascular response

Any trauma to the skin that penetrates the dermis will result in bleeding. The damaged ends of blood vessels immediately constrict in order to minimise blood loss. The exposure of blood to the air helps to initiate the clotting process which is accelerated owing to platelet aggregation (Figure 1).

A blood clot is produced by a complex chain reaction called the coagulation cascade. This is characterised by the formation of a fibrin mesh which temporarily closes the wound and gradually dries out to become a scab.

At this stage, wounds usually produce large amounts of blood and serous fluid which help to cleanse the wound of surface contaminants (Tortora and Grabowski, 1996).

The inflammatory response

Tissue damage and the activation of clotting factors during the vascular phase stimulates the release of inflammatory mediators such as prostaglandins and histamine from cells such as mast cells. These mediators cause blood vessels adjacent to the injured area to become more permeable and to vasodilate.

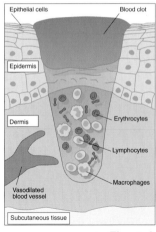

Figures 1–4: Flanagan, M. (1997)
Wound Management.
Edinburgh: Churchill Livingstone.

Figure 1

This inflammatory response occurs rapidly and can be detected by the presence of localised heat, swelling, erythema, discomfort and functional disturbance (Tortora and Grabowski, 1996).

Inflammation is part of the body's normal protective response to injury and, although the clinical signs are similar, should not be confused with the presence of wound infection. The classic signs of inflammation are due to increased blood flow to the area and the accumulation of fluid in the soft tissues. The combination of discomfort and swelling usually restricts function.

Wound exudate is produced during this stage of healing owing to the increased permeability of the capillary membranes. Exudate contains proteins and a variety of nutrients, growth factors and enzymes which facilitate healing. It also has antimicrobial properties (Hutchinson, 1989).

Exudate production, which is most prolific during the inflammatory phase of healing, bathes the wound with nutrients and actively cleanses the wound surface. It also acts as a growth medium for phagocytic cells (Katz et al, 1991). However, excessive exudate production can cause skin sensitivities and tissue maceration.

Neutrophils are the first type of white blood cell to be attracted into the wound, usually arriving within a few hours of injury. These phagocytic cells have a short life span but provide initial protection against micro-organisms as they engulf and digest foreign bodies (Clark, 1988).

After two to three days, macrophages become the predominant leukocyte in the wound bed. Their function at this stage is to cleanse the wound. Macrophages are present throughout all stages of the healing process, producing a variety of substances that regulate healing including growth factors, prostaglandins and complement factors (complex proteins) (Nathan, 1987).

The inflammatory phase is a precursor to subsequent stages of wound healing. Patients who are immunosuppressed are often unable to produce a typical inflammatory response and may therefore fail to activate the normal healing process (Baxter, 1994).

In clean wounds, the inflammatory phase can last from three to seven days (Dyson et al, 1988). In necrotic or clinically infected wounds this process is prolonged. Slough formation is common during the inflammatory stage and occurs when a collection of dead cellular debris accumulates on the wound surface. It may be creamy yellow in colour owing to the large amounts of leukocytes present. Chronic wounds in particular may develop areas of fibrous tissue that cover the base of the wound. This often combines with slough, making it harder to remove.

Formation of new tissue in the wound bed will not occur until the macrophages have stimulated the proliferative phase by the release of growth factors and the wound bed has been sufficiently cleansed by the inflammatory process (Robson, 1997). Macrophages are responsible for controlling the transition between the inflammatory and proliferative phases of healing (Diegelmann et al, 1991).

The proliferative stage

During this phase the wound is filled with new connective tissue. A decrease in wound size is achieved by a combination of the physiological processes of granulation, contraction and epithelialisation. Granulation occurs first, followed by the combined effects of wound contraction and re-epithelialisation (Figures 2 and 3).

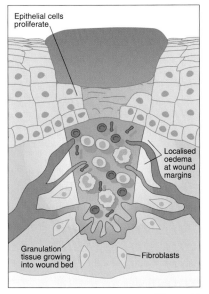

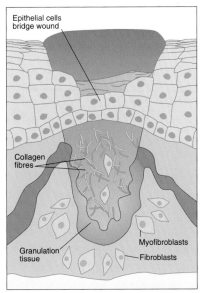

| **Figure 2** | **Figure 3** |

The formation of granulation tissue

Granulation is the term used to describe the new wound matrix, which is made up of collagen and an extracellular material called ground substance. These provide the scaffolding into which new capillaries will grow.

The growth of new blood vessels is termed angiogenesis. This is stimulated by macrophage activity and tissue hypoxia resulting from the disruption of blood flow at time of injury. The role of oxygen in wound healing is complex and not yet fully understood. It may be significantly different in epidermal and connective tissue repair (Knighton et al, 1981).

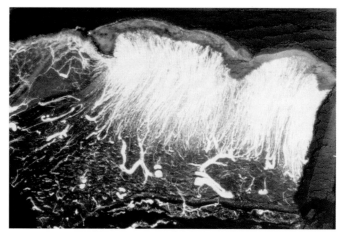

An X-ray showing angiogenesis in an acute wound

Macrophages produce a variety of substances that stimulate angiogenesis and the synthesis of collagen by fibroblasts. These include transforming growth factor (TGF), which promotes formation of new tissue and blood vessels, and tumour necrosing factor (TNF), which facilitates the breakdown of necrotic tissue, stimulating proliferation (Nathan, 1987).

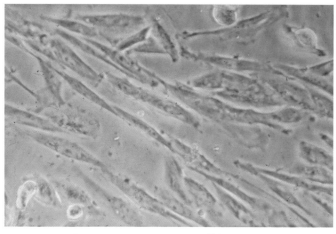

Fibroblasts in a petri dish

Granulation tissue is so called because its appearance is granular and slightly uneven. Healthy granulation tissue does not bleed easily and is a pinky-red colour. The condition of granulation tissue is often a good indicator as to how the wound is healing. Granulation tissue which is dark in colour may signal that the wound is ischaemic or infected (Harding and Cutting, 1994).

Wound contraction

After connective tissue production, fibroblasts congregate around the wound margin. They contract, pulling the edges of the wound together. This does not occur to any great extent in sutured wounds, where there is minimal tissue loss, but does play a significant part in the healing of large, open wounds (Brown, 1988).

Re-epithelialisation

The regrowth of epithelial cells across the wound surface occurs during the final stage of proliferation (Figure 4).

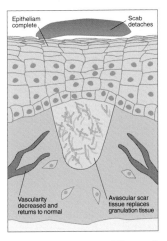

Figure 4

A moist wound environment accelerates this process, enabling epithelial cells to migrate more easily (Winter, 1962). The progress of epithelial migration is significantly slowed in the presence of either necrotic tissue or a scab, as epithelial cells are forced to burrow underneath the escar which forms a mechanical obstruction in the wound bed. The mitotic activity of cells within a wound is sensitive to local fluctuations in temperature and is significantly slowed down at temperature extremes (Lock, 1979; Myers, 1982).

In wounds healing by secondary intention, epithelialisation occurs once granulation tissue fills the wound bed. New epithelial cells, which have a translucent appearance and are usually whitish-pink in colour, originate from either the wound margin or from the remnants of hair follicles, sebaceous or sweat glands. They divide and migrate along the surface of the granulation tissue until they form a continuous layer (Garrett, 1998). Small islands of epithelial cells within a wound can be difficult to identify, especially if they are hidden by slough, fibrous tissue or exudate.

The maturation stage

In healthy individuals this stage begins approximately 20 days after injury and can last for many months or even years in complex wounds (Clark, 1988). Initially scar tissue is raised and reddish in colour. As the scar matures, its blood supply decreases and it becomes flatter, paler and smoother. In darkly pigmented skin, the colour of scar tissue is usually lighter than the surrounding skin.

Mature scar tissue is avascular and contains no hairs, sebaceous or sweat glands. Scar formation is a normal consequence of the process of tissue repair in adults. Foetal wounds have been shown to heal without the production of scar tissue (Whitby and Ferguson, 1991).

Remodelling of scar tissue is stimulated by macrophages and results in the reorganisation of collagen fibres to maximise tensile strength (Diegelmann et al, 1991). The tensile strength of scar tissue compared to normal skin is about 80% (Brown, 1988).

The formation of keloid and hypertrophic (raised) scars are abnormalities associated with this stage of healing. Hypertrophic scarring occurs directly after initial repair, while keloid scarring may occur some time after healing (Eisenbeiss et al, 1998). Keloid scars continue to grow and spread, invading surrounding healthy tissue, whereas hypertrophic scars do not. Black Afro-Caribbean people are 10 times more likely to develop keloid scarring than Caucasians (Lee, 1982).

Delayed wound healing

Many wounds heal without incident. However, there are many factors that can significantly delay healing. Often the exact mechanism of delay is not well understood and requires further investigation (Flanagan, 1997). The general health of an individual has a direct influence on their ability to heal normally and chronic diseases affect wound healing in a multitude of different ways.

Conditions resulting in reduced tissue perfusion, metabolic disturbances or malabsorbtion syndromes contribute to delayed repair (Fincham-Gee, 1990).

Local factors such as wound infection, mechanical stress, use of toxic cleansing agents and the presence of foreign bodies can also prolong healing (Krasnor, 1996). Finally, socio-economic and psychological factors can also have a detrimental effect on the rate of repair (Kiecolt-Glaser et al, 1995).

Conclusion

Nursing skills are challenged by patients with non-healing chronic wounds which can have a profound effect on the quality of an individual's life. To maximise wound healing potential, practitioners need to relate their knowledge of wound physiology to everyday clinical practice. Nurses are in a unique position within the multidisciplinary team to assess patients' wounds. In doing so they should take account of the delicate balance between the physical and psycho-social influences that can affect healing.

References

Baxter, C.R. (1994) Immunologic reactions in chronic wounds. *American Journal of Surgery*; 167: supplement, 12S–14S.

Bennett, G., Moody, M. (1995) *Wound Care for Health Professionals.* London: Chapman and Hall.

Brown, G.L. (1988) Acceleration of tensile strength of incisions treated with EGF and TGF. *Annals of Surgery*; 208, 788–794.

Clark, R.A.F. (1988) Overview and general considerations of wound repair. In: Clark, R.A.F, Henson, P.M. (eds) *The Molecular and Cellular Biology of Wound Repair.* New York: Plenum.

Diegelmann, R. et al (1991) The role of macrophages in wound repair: a review. *Plastic Reconstructive Surgery*; 68: 107–113.

Dyson, M. et al (1988) Comparison of the effects of moist and dry conditions on dermal repair. *Journal of Investigative Dermatology*; 91: 5, 435–439.

Eisenbeiss, W. et al (1998) Hypertrophic scars and keloids. *Journal of Wound Care*; 7: 5, 255–257.

Fincham-Gee, C. (1990) Nutrition and wound healing. *Nursing*; 4: 18, 26–28.

Flanagan, M. (1997) *Wound Management.* Edinburgh: Churchill Livingstone.

Garrett, B. (1998) Re-epithelialisation. *Journal of Wound Care*; 7: 7, 358–359.

Harding, K., Cutting, K. (1994) Criteria for identifying wound infection. *Journal of Wound Care*; 3: 4, 198–201.

Hutchinson, J.J. (1989) Prevalence of wound infection under occlusive dressings: a collective survey of reported research. *Wounds*; 1: 123–133.

Katz, M.H. et al (1991) Human wound fluid from acute wounds stimulates fibroblasts and endothelial cell growth. *Journal of American Academic Dermatology*; 25: 1054–1058.

Kiecolt-Glaser, J.K. et al (1995) Slowing of wound healing by psychological stress. *Lancet*; 346, 1194–1196.

Knighton, D. et al (1981) Regulation of wound healing angiogenesis: effect of oxygen gradients and inspired oxygen concentration. *Surgery*; 90: 262–270.

Krasnor, D. (1996) *Chronic Wound Care: A Clinical Sourcebook for Healthcare Professionals* (2nd edition). Philadelphia: Health Management Publications.

Lee, C.P. (1982) Keloids: their epidemiology and treatment. *International Journal of Dermatology*; 21: 9, 504–505.

Lock, P. (1979) *The Effects of Temperature on Mitotic Activity at the Edge of Experimental Wounds.* (Lock Research Laboratories Paper). Kent: Lock Laboratories.

Myers, J.A. (1982) Wound healing and the use of a modern surgical dressing. *Pharmaceutical Journal*; 2: 103–104.

Nathan, C.F. (1987) Secretory products of macrophages. *Journal of Clinical Investigation*; 79: 319–326.

Robson, M.C. (1997) The role of growth factors in the healing of chronic wounds. *Wound Repair and Regeneration*; 5: 12–17.

Tortora, G.J., Grabowski, S.R. (1996) *Principles of Anatomy and Physiology* (8th edition). New York: Harper Collins College Publications.

Winter, G. (1962) Formulation of the scab and the rate of epithelialisation in the skin of the domestic pig. *Nature*; 193: 293–294.

Winter, G., Scales, J.T. (1963) Effect of air drying and dressings on the surface of a wound. *Nature*; 5: 91–92.

Whitby, D.J., Ferguson, M.W. (1991) Immunohistochemical localisation of growth factors in foetal healing. *Developmental Biology*; 147: 207–215.

3 Wound assessment

Mick Miller

Key points

▶ Thorough assessment, correct diagnosis and effective documentation is essential in order to treat wounds effectively

▶ Assessment should include identification of all factors that may delay healing

▶ Specific diagnosis of the underlying cause of a wound can be ascertained from clinical signs and appropriate investigations

▶ Other factors that should be assessed include current care and local wound environment

Introduction

We all make hundreds, possibly thousands, of assessments every day, many of them without conscious thought. The simple task of deciding on the best moment to pull out into traffic when driving is based on multiple and complex assessments of speed, time and distance. Most drivers carry out this procedure without too much conscious consideration. But if the assessment is not thorough and they fail to spot a car approaching from another junction, the result may be a serious accident.

Wound assessment can be likened to pulling out on to a busy roundabout. It is about gathering data before you act. Just as a quick glance before speeding into traffic may have disastrous results, inadequate wound assessment can lead to incorrect or inadequate treatment, with serious consequences. For example, applying compression bandaging to an ulcer assumed to be venous when severe arterial disease exists may result in limb loss.

Benner (1984) demonstrated that seemingly intuitive decisions made by expert nurses actually result from a complex decision-making process developed over years of experience. Because of this experience, expert nurses can quickly identify issues relevant to patient care. Benner also showed that nurses who do not have this level of expertise in a particular field need to follow a logical and systematic plan to ensure that all relevant aspects are taken into account. If an assessment follows a pre-planned structure, it is more likely that the patient will receive appropriate treatment.

There are various frameworks for wound assessment. Some authors have suggested basing assessment on existing nursing models (Dealey, 1994; Bale and Jones, 1997). Others use conceptual diagrams to illustrate the relationships between the different factors that influence wound healing (Bale and Morison, 1997; Harding, 1992).

The method presented here approaches assessment by asking two simple questions (Miller, 1995):

▶ What factors are interfering with wound healing?

▶ Which of these can be changed to help move the wound on to the next phase of repair?

Factors delaying healing

These can be found in three main areas:

▶ general health

▶ care being given

▶ the local wound environment

The wound itself is last on the list because it is the last place practitioners should look when gathering clues as to why the healing process may be delayed.

General health

There are many reasons why the patient's general health and health circumstances may affect wound healing. If these are not identified and resolved, where possible, the patient is unlikely to experience optimum repair no matter what issues are identified and addressed relevant to the local wound environment. Two main areas need to be assessed with reference to the patient's general health: associated health issues and specific aetiology.

Associated health issues

This refers to any factors which may affect a patient's chance of healing, no matter what the specific aetiology of their wound. These factors include:

▶ age

▶ social environment

▶ psychological perspective

▶ nutrition

▶ associated disease processes (particularly those which reduce oxygen supply to the wound or result in mobility and/or sensation loss)

▶ certain drug therapies

▶ infection

▶ diabetes

▶ care environment

▶ history of occurrence.

Some of these factors may also be related to the specific aetiology of the wound type.

Age

The skin's capacity to repair reduces with age (Desai, 1997). This suggests that elderly people will take longer to heal, although no specific research is available to indicate how much delay can be expected at what age. Aged skin contains less collagen and has reduced elasticity. Because of this, it may be less able to withstand mechanical insult, making it more prone to tissue damage (Lauker et al, 1986).

Fibroblasts which synthesise collagen decrease in number as skin ages, which accounts for the diminished collagen content (Tortora and Anagnostakos, 1990). Phagocytic cells, such as macrophages, become less efficient, which has implications for elderly people's ability to combat bacterial colonisation (Eaglestein, 1986). Elderly people are also more likely to have associated disease and to be malnourished (Lewis, 1997).

Collagen in healthy skin

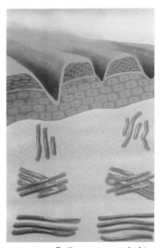

Collagen in aged skin

BSIP/Science Photo Library

Social factors

Research suggests there is a strong link between social circumstance and health. The Black report (1982) found that people in the lowest of five social groupings were almost twice as likely to become ill or die than those in the highest group.

It is likely that social conditions also have an effect on wound healing. People from a poorer social environment may eat a less nutritious diet. Smoking also impairs healing by reducing oxygen availability to damaged tissue (Siana and Gottrup, 1992).

Psychological factors

One study published in 1976 (Felton et al) demonstrated that patients who were psychologically prepared before surgery had better health outcomes than those who were not. This suggests that patients who understand their care may heal better.

Stress has been implicated as a causative factor in many disease processes and may contribute to poor wound healing. A study by Kiecolt-Glaser et al (1995) showed that punch biopsy wounds in women under stress (caring for relatives with Alzheimer's disease) took significantly longer to heal (48.7 days) than biopsy sites on control subjects (39.9 days).

Nutrition

Proteins, carbohydrates, vitamins and minerals are all involved in wound healing (McLaren, 1992; Pinchcofsky-Devin, 1994). It is probable that a higher-than-average daily intake of these components is needed for optimal wound repair and that a reduced intake interferes with healing (Gilmore et al, 1995).

Associated disease processes

Some disease processes have a negative effect on wound repair. Human tissue needs oxygen to heal. Factors that reduce the supply of oxygen to a wound, such as cardiac disease, anaemia or chronic breathing problems, are likely to delay healing (Roberts et al, 1994; Byl and Hopf, 1995).

The majority of a wound's oxygen supply is provided via the underlying blood circulation (Silver, 1985). It has been shown that a hypoxic environment can stimulate blood vessel proliferation (angiogenesis) in acute animal wounds (Cherry and Ryan, 1985). But it is questionable whether these findings can be applied to chronic ulcers, which are often caused or exacerbated by poor oxygen delivery (Leaper and Harding, 1998) and are likely to be chronically hypoxic.

Illnesses that result in loss of sensation and movement, such as cerebrovascular accidents and neck of femur fractures, increase the risk of pressure damage. Healing will also be delayed by any blockage of the blood supply to damaged tissue (Anthony, 1996).

Other diseases may cause ulceration. Rheumatoid arthritis, for example, is associated with the development of leg ulcers in about 10% of cases (Morison and Moffatt, 1997). Underlying disease such as this may complicate healing.

Drug therapies

Steroids have been shown to inhibit collagen synthesis, reduce tensile strength and retard wound healing (McCulloch et al, 1995; Hunt et al, 1969). Other drugs cited as impairing normal wound healing are non-steroid anti-inflammatory drugs, immunosuppressive agents, anticoagulants and antiprostaglandins (McCulloch et al, 1995).

Infection

Although numbers and types of bacteria are factors in the occurrence of wound infection, there is evidence that many venous ulcers and pressure ulcers can tolerate high levels of bacteria and still heal normally (Gilchrist and Reed, 1989; Alinovi et al, 1986).

Many UK practitioners agree that the definition of infection ultimately pivots around how the individual patient responds to bacteria and not how many or what type of bacteria are present (Miller and Gilchrist, 1997; Ayton, 1985).

In the USA, it is thought that a bacteria level above 10^5 per gram of tissue constitutes infection (Krizek et al, 1967; Robson, 1976; Heggers, 1998). But much of the work supporting this theory was undertaken on patients with surgical or acute injuries, which are not relevant to chronic wounds (Thomson and Smith, 1994). Even some surgical studies have demonstrated that many patients with bacterial levels greater than 10^5 heal normally (Robson et al, 1973).

Whether or not infection can be defined by the number of bacteria present, a host response to bacteria such as erythema or cellulitis can be indicative of a delay in healing. Infection will need to be resolved before healing will continue.

Diabetes mellitus

Diabetes mellitus is linked to disease processes such as peripheral neuropathy and arteriosclerosis, which can lead to ulceration. Diabetes has also been shown to delay wound healing generally. These effects are due to secondary physiological changes such as reduction in tissue collagen, defective granulocyte function, defective cell chemotaxis and reduced capillary in-growth (Silhi, 1998).

Care environment

Different facilities and expertise are available depending on where care is being provided. A hospital clinic may have access to measurement techniques such as Duplex™ colour scanning and to people with particular expertise such as vascular and diabetic specialists.

But care is more frequently provided in the community, where immediate access to specialist knowledge and facilities may be limited. In both hospital and community settings, the nurse's ability to provide optimum care may be constrained by a lack of resources such as pressure-redistributing mattresses and hoists.

History of occurrence

A history of when and how the wound first occurred provides important information, particularly in the case of acute, traumatic wounds. When caring for a patient with a serious traumatic injury, the first priority is always airway, breathing and circulation. Once the patient is stable, further wound assessment can be undertaken. In the case of both major and minor traumatic wounds, an accurate history of the mechanism of injury is vital. This will provide an idea of wound depth, the likelihood of foreign bodies remaining in the wound and the degree of possible contamination.

In the case of a chronic wound, the history of occurrence should provide some information to aid diagnosis. History of effectiveness of past care may also provide useful information to guide future treatment.

Using the information

It may not be possible or prudent to change some factors which affect healing, such as age and concomitant drug therapy. It is still important, however, to identify these during assessment and recognise that they may negatively affect tissue repair. This will enable both nurse and patient to form a realistic idea of healing potential.

Calculating the degree of affect each factor has in delaying wound healing is a challenge that remains for clinicians and scientists.

Some factors can be changed. The patient may be encouraged to stop smoking or improve their diet. The incentive of potentially healing their leg ulcer can be strong enough motivation for a patient to change long-standing behaviour patterns. The involvement of other health professionals, such as social workers, can help improve a patient's social environment.

Factors such as the patient's psychological state and the environment in which care is provided can also be improved by the nurse. A good adage is: change what you can but recognise and acknowledge what you can't.

Specific underlying cause

After identifying general issues that interfere with healing, it is vital to determine specific underlying causes. This will directly affect the care given. The treatment for someone with a venous ulcer, for example, will be very different to the treatment given to a patient with an arterial ulcer. If the specific underlying cause is not identified and rectified, wound healing will be impaired.

Fortunately, most wounds produce tell-tale signs of underlying aetiology. These are covered in specific chapters, but, as an example, venous leg ulcers tend to be large, wet and shallow with sloping edges while arterial ulcers tend to be small, dry and relatively deep with 'punched out' edges. The assessor must be able to identify and understand the significance of signs associated with each wound type.

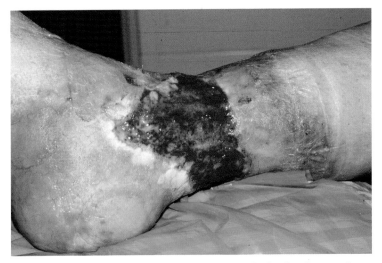

A typical venous ulcer over the medial malleolus. It is large and wet with sloping edges. Lipodermatosclerosis is also present.

If clinicians are unsure about underlying pathophysiology, patients should be referred for further assessment. At the end of the process, the assessor should have all the information needed to make a differential diagnosis. Until the underlying cause of the wound is diagnosed, effective treatment will not be possible.

Diagnosis becomes more difficult when the wound is caused by more than one contributing disease. Co-existing arterial disease, for example, can be found in venous and neuropathic ulcers. An ankle brachial pressure index (ABPI) will provide some indication as to the existence and extent of arterial deficit. In hospital, tests such as colour Duplex™ scanning and arteriography can be undertaken to assess vascular patency. If the assessor is unsure, further advice should be sought.

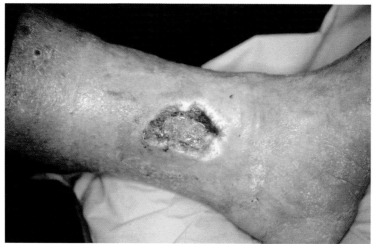

A mixed venous/arterial ulcer

Some ulcers are caused by relatively uncommon conditions such as pyoderma gangrenousum or malignancy. If an ulcer shows no sign of healing or rapidly deteriorates with accepted therapy, referral for further diagnostic tests, such as biopsy, is recommended.

Assessing the care

It may be that certain aspects of current care are a barrier to optimal healing. These include:

- ▶ not addressing the underlying cause

- ▶ using dry dressings

- ▶ not managing wound exudate

- ▶ not removing devitalised tissue from the wound

- ▶ using a dressing inappropriately

Not addressing the underlying cause

If the wound itself is the primary focus for assessment, care may be based on a subjective appraisal of the wound bed, followed by a choice of which dressing to use. If underlying cause and health issues preventing healing are not identified and addressed, the patient will have a reduced chance of their wound repairing.

Dry dressings

It is now accepted that simple dressings, such as gauze and paraffin gauze, do not provide optimal healing in many situations (Turner, 1985; Field and Kerstein, 1994). A moist wound environment has been shown to increase epithelialisation and stimulate proliferation in experimental and human acute wounds (Winter, 1962; Alvarez et al, 1983; Dyson et al, 1988; Hinman and Maibach, 1963; Field and Kerstein, 1994).

Modern dressings, such as foams, gels and hydrocolloids, keep the wound bed moist (Thomas, 1990). Although these dressings are more expensive per item than traditional materials, their use leads to savings when all elements of care are accounted for. This is mostly because fewer dressing changes are needed (Fanucci and Seese, 1991; Mulder, 1995; Colwell et al, 1993).

There are some situations where a moist wound product may not be appropriate. These include diabetic ulcers and ischaemic digits.

Managing wound exudate

A moist wound/dressing interface provides an optimum environment for healing, but if the wound and surrounding tissues become wet and macerated the patient is at risk of further wound breakdown (Miller and Collier, 1996). It is important that a dressing is able to remove excess exudate and keep it away from the wound bed.

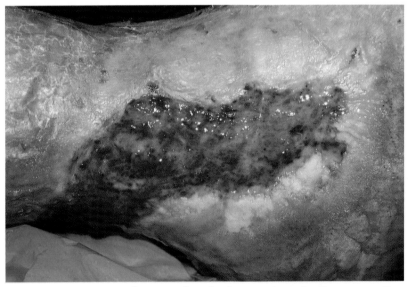

A venous ulcer that is too wet, causing tissue maceration

Not removing devitalised tissue from the wound

A significant amount of dead tissue covering the wound prevents progression into the proliferative phase of healing. It may make the wound more prone to infection and obscure the wound bed, making accurate assessment of wound size and depth impossible.

Using a dressing inappropriately

Before using any dressing, the nurse must read the instructions. Using dressings on wounds they are not designed for may interfere with healing. For example, some alginates need a reasonable amount of exudate to gel; if used on wounds that are too dry they will stick and not be effective.

Assessing the wound

Local wound assessment provides information relevant to three areas:

▶ type of wound

▶ stage of wound healing

▶ increase or decrease in wound size

Type

Wound size, position, depth and exudate level will assist clinical diagnosis. Venous leg ulcers, for instance, tend to be situated around the medial malleolus and are large, shallow and highly exudating.

Stage

The condition of the wound bed and local wound environment will provide information about the stage of healing. If the tissue in the wound is predominately necrotic or sloughy, or if is infected, the wound is likely to be in the inflammatory phase of healing. Granulation and epithelial tissue are evidence of proliferation.

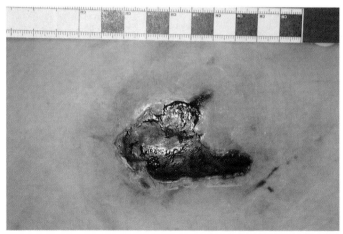

Hard black necrotic tissue

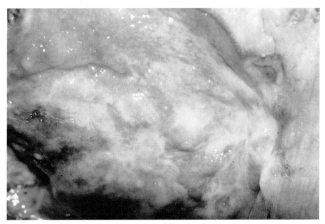

Fibrinous yellow slough in the base of a pressure ulcer

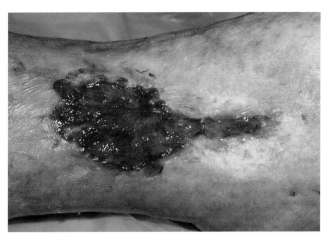

New granulation tissue in the bed of a healing venous ulcer

New epithelial tissue covering a freshly healed acute wound

Size

Ultimately, wound healing is demonstrated by a reduction in wound size. The easiest way to measure this is to assess wound surface area by multiplying greatest breadth by greatest length.

Wound tracing is also useful and acetate grids are available for this purpose. They are laid across the wound so that the edges can be traced and its area measured. If the wound is traced it is also a good idea to trace around any particular area of defined tissue existing within the wound (such as necrotic, granulating or epithelial). If the amount of necrotic material in the wound is decreasing, for instance, this would indicate progress towards healing.

Photography is another measurement method. There are cameras that use film with a grid which can be used to estimate wound area. Photography also provides a record of the type and extent of tissue covering the wound.

Documentation

Formal assessment charts are useful because they help to ensure that all relevant areas are covered during assessment. They also provide a guide to documenting findings.

Effective documentation is obviously important, both as a record and to ensure continuity of care. The key to effective documentation is the use of commonly understood language. If something is described in terms that do not have common meaning, the next person providing care may form a different conclusion to that which was originally meant. Even an apparently innocuous term such as 'medium amount of exudate' can be confusing, as nurses may have different ideas of what the term 'medium' means depending on their experience.

Summary

Assessment needs to identify both the general health issues which affect healing and the specific underlying pathology causing the wound. Current care also needs to be appraised for appropriateness and effectiveness. Lastly, the appearance of the wound and wound bed should be assessed and measured.

All findings should be documented in a clear manner using terminology that is commonly accepted and understood. When assessment is logical and systematic, it optimises the patient's chances of healing.

References

Alinovi, A. et al (1986) Systemic administration of antibiotics in the management of venous ulcers: a randomised clinical trial. *Journal of the American Academy of Dermatology*; 15: 186–191.

Alvarez, O.M. et al (1983) The effect of occlusive dressings on collagen synthesis and re-epithelialisation in superficial wounds. *Journal of Surgical Research*; 35: 142–148.

Anthony, D.M. (1996) The formation of pressure sores and the role of nursing care. *Journal of Wound Care*; 5: 4, 192–194.

Ayton, M. (1985) Wounds that won't heal. *Nursing Times (Community Outlook* supplement); 81: 46, 16–19.

Bale, S., Jones, V. (1997) *Wound Care Nursing: A Patient-Centred Approach.* London: Baillière Tindall.

Bale, S., Morison, M. (1997) Patient assessment. In: Morison, M. et al *A Colour Guide to the Nursing Management of Chronic Wounds* (2nd edition). London: C.V. Mosby.

Benner, P. (1984) *From Novice to Expert.* California: Addison-Wesley.

Black, D. (1982) *Inequalities in Health* (Black Report) Harmondsworth: Penguin.

Byl, N.N., Hopf, H. (1995) The use of oxygen in wound healing. In: McCulloch, J.M. et al (eds) *Wound Healing: Alternatives in Management* (2nd edition). Philadelphia: F.A. Davis.

Cherry, G.W., Ryan, T.J. (1985) Enhanced wound angiogenesis with a new hydrocolloid dressing. In: Ryan, T.J. (ed.) *An Environment for Healing: The Role of Occlusion (Proceedings of a Wound Care Symposium).* International Congress and Symposium Series No. 88. London: Royal Society of Medicine.

Colwell, J.C. et al (1993) A comparison of the efficacy and cost-effectiveness of two methods of managing pressure ulcers. *Decubitus*; 6: 4, 28–36.

Dealey, C. (1994) *The Care of Wounds.* Oxford: Blackwell.

Desai, H. (1997) Ageing and wounds: Part 2. Healing in old age. *Journal of Wound Care*; 6: 5, 237–239.

Dyson, M. et al (1988) Comparison of the effects of moist and dry conditions on dermal repair. *Journal of Investigative Dermatology*; 91: 5, 435–439.

Eaglestein, W.H. (1986) Wound healing and ageing. *Dermatologic Clinics*; 4: 481–484

Fanucci, D., Seese, J. (1991) Multi-faceted use of calcium alginates: a painless, cost effective alternative for wound care management. *Ostomy Wound Management*; 37: 16–22.

Felton, G. et al (1976) Preoperative nursing intervention with the patient for surgery: outcomes of three alternative approaches. *International Journal of Nursing Studies*; 13: 83–86.

Field, C. K., Kerstein, M.D. (1994) Overview of wound healing in a moist environment. *American Journal of Surgery*; 167: 1a (supplement), S2–S6.

Gilchrist, B., Reed, C. (1989) The bacteriology of chronic venous leg ulcers treated with occlusive hydrocolloid dressings. *British Journal of Dermatology*; 121: 337–344.

Gilmore, S.A. et al (1995) Clinical indicators associated with unintentional weight loss and pressure ulcers in elderly residents of nursing facilities. *Journal of the American Diatetic Association*; 95: 984–992.

Harding, K. (1992) *The Wound Programme*. Dundee: Centre for Medical Education.

Heggers, J.P. (1998) Defining infection in chronic wounds: does it matter? *Journal of Wound Care*; 7: 8, 389–392.

Hinman, C.D., Maibach, H. (1963) Effects of air exposure and occlusion on experimental human skin wounds. *Nature*; 200: 377–378.

Hunt, T. K. et al (1969) The effect of vitamin A on reversing the inhibitory effect of cortisone in the healing of open wounds. *American Surgery*; 170: 633–641.

Kiecolt-Glaser J.K. et al (1995) Slowing of wound healing by psychological stress. *Lancet*; 346: 1194–1196.

Krizek, T.J. et al (1967) Bacterial growth and skin survival. *Surgical Forum*; 18: 518.

Lauker et al (1986) Morphology of aged skin. *Dermatologic Clinics*; 1986; 4: 379–389

Leaper, D.J., Harding, K.G. (1998) *Wounds: Biology and Management*. New York: Oxford Medical Publications.

Lewis, B. (1997) Nutrition and age in the aetiology of pressure sores. *Journal of Wound Care*; 6: 1, 41–42.

McCulloch, J.M. et al (eds) (1995) *Wound Healing: Alternatives in Management* (2nd edition). Philadelphia: F.A. Davis.

McLaren, S.G.M. (1992) Nutrition and wound healing. *Journal of Wound Care*; 1: 3, 45–55.

Miller, M. (1995) Principles of wound assessment. *Emergency Nurse*; 3: 1, 16–18.

Miller, M., Collier, C. (1996) *Understanding Wounds*. London: Macmillan.

Miller, M., Gilchrist, B. (1997) *Understanding Wound Cleaning and Infection*. London: Macmillan.

Morison, M., Moffatt, (1997) C. Leg ulcers In: Morison, M. et al *A Colour Guide to the Nursing Management of Chronic Wounds*. London: C.V. Mosby.

Mulder, G.D. (1995) Cost-effective managed care: gel versus wet-to-dry for debridement. *Ostomy Wound Management*; 41: 68–74.

Pinchcofsky-Devin, G. (1994) Nutrition and wound healing. *Journal of Wound Care*; 3: 5, 231–234.

Roberts, G.W. et al (1994) The effects of hyperbaric oxygen on cultured fibroblasts. *Journal of Wound Care*; 3: 4, 189–193.

Robson, M.C. et al (1973) Rapid bacterial screening in the treatment of civilian wounds. *Journal of Surgical Research*; 14: 420–430.

Robson, M. (1976) Management of the contaminated wound: aids in diagnosis and treatment. In: Krizek, T., Hoops, J. (eds) *Symposium on Basic Sciences in Plastic Surgery*. St Louis: C.V. Mosby.

Siana, J.E., Gottrup, F. (1992) The effects of smoking on tissue function. *Journal of Wound Care*; 1: 2, 37–41.

Silhi, N. (1998) A review of the diabetes-related factors that affect wound healing. *Journal of Wound Care*; 7: 1, 47–51.

Silver, I. A. (1985) Oxygen and tissue repair. In: Ryan, T. J. (ed.) *An Environment for Healing: The Role of Occlusion (Proceedings of a Wound Care Symposium).* International Congress and Symposium Series No. 88. London: Royal Society of Medicine.

Thomas, S. (1990) *Wound Management and Dressings.* London: Pharmaceutical Press.

Thompson, P.D., Smith, D.J. (1994) What is infection? *American Journal of Surgery*; 167: 1a (supplement), S7–S11.

Tortora, G.J., Anagnostakos, N.P. (1990) *Principles of Anatomy and Physiology.* New York: Harper and Row.

Turner, T.D. (1985) Which dressing and why? In: Westaby, S. (ed.) *Wound Care.* London: Heinemann.

Winter, G.D. (1962) Formation of the scab and the rate of epithelization of superficial wounds in the skin of the young domestic pig. *Nature*; 193: 293–294.

4 Traumatic wounds: principles of management

Michael C.R. Whiteside
Robert John Moorehead

Key points

▶ The extent of the force determines the nature of the injury

▶ Wounds can be classified as tidy or untidy

▶ General principles of wound management cover blood supply, debridement, irrigation, exploration, antibiotics and tetanus

▶ Decisions about wound closure are based on judgement and experience

Introduction

A surgeon dealing with traumatic injuries will encounter a wide variety of wounds. The spectrum is vast, ranging from minor cuts and abrasions to extensive tissue injuries which can be life-threatening. The extent of the force that causes the wound determines the nature of the injury, therefore the circumstances of the traumatic injury together with the nature and site of the defect guide the surgeon towards appropriate management decisions.

A traumatic wound occurs when the body is subjected to a force that exceeds the strength of the skin or underlying supporting tissues. In practical terms traumatic wounds can be classified as tidy or untidy.

In general terms a tidy wound has a clean incision, is uncontaminated, is less than six hours old and is caused by low-energy trauma. Conversely an untidy wound has an irregular ragged edge, is more than 12 hours old, is contaminated and is usually caused by high-energy trauma.

Initial management

A major wound is not immediately life-threatening unless there is serious haemorrhage leading to exsanguination. Severe wounds must not distract emergency staff from the first priorities of treatment; that is, the normal resuscitation protocol, ensuring an adequate airway, optimising ventilation and restoring circulatory volume.

After resuscitation a good history is useful, either from the patient or a witness to the incident. This will help determine how the injury occurred and will give a guide to the degree of force that caused the wound, the possibility of contamination and the likelihood of other injuries.

Careful examination is required to identify all injuries. Apparently minor injuries must not be neglected as these can result in long-term disability or disfigurement.

General principles of management

The management of a traumatic wound requires adherence to certain basic principles to achieve a successful outcome (Rosen and Cleary, 1991).

Blood supply

Injured tissue needs an adequate blood supply for the wound to heal. In limb injuries the competence of the circulation must be assessed. Local contusion, penetrating injuries, fractures and major joint dislocations may occlude or divide blood vessels. If such an injury is suspected it should be treated promptly.

Debridement

All necrotic or devitalised tissue must be debrided. This is considered the single most important factor in managing a contaminated wound (Haury et al, 1978). Debridement has two benefits. First, it removes tissue that is contaminated with dirt and bacteria and removes devitalised tissue which improves the wound's ability to resist infection. Identifying all devitalised tissue can be extremely difficult, but muscle viability can be assessed by contractility, bleeding, colour and consistency.

Second, devitalised soft tissue acts as a culture medium for bacterial growth and the anaerobic environment will decrease leukocyte activity, so its removal has obvious benefits for healing. Host defences against invading bacteria are reduced by foreign bodies in a wound.

Irrigation

Irrigation is necessary to remove contaminants and haematomas which provide a culture medium for the proliferation of bacteria. Manual scrubbing of a wound will cause a local increase in tissue oedema and therefore decrease host defences. But vigorous cleaning with soap and water may be necessary to remove road grease, carbon and dirt which, if left, can lead to unsightly tattooing.

Exploration

Wounds need to be explored to allow adequate debridement and cleaning and to identify damage to deep structures (McNicholl et al, 1992). This should be carried out under either local or general anaesthesia. Vessel, tendon and nerve injuries are repaired as appropriate to restore function. In relatively tidy wounds, primary repair of tendons and nerves may be possible. In untidy wounds, however, it is advisable simply to identify the proximal and distal ends and mark them with a suture for repair at a later stage.

Antibiotics and tetanus

Antibiotic and tetanus prophylaxis should be administered as appropriate. Prophylactic antibiotics are valuable when the wound is heavily contaminated or if host resistance is compromised, for example, in patients with impaired circulation, diabetes, leukaemia or those taking immunosuppressive drugs. However, antibiotic treatment must not replace adequate debridement and cleaning. Tetanus caused by *Clostridium tetani,* an anaerobic organism, requires devitalised tissue for growth.

Debridement of all dead tissue is the best prophylaxis against tetanus. The risk is very low in a clean or adequately debrided wound. The patient's tetanus immunisation state should be ascertained and, if necessary, a booster dose of detoxified toxin administered. Patients with heavily contaminated wounds may require passive immunisation with anti-tetanus globulin injection.

Vascular injuries

The duration of limb ischaemia following trauma to a major vessel is one of several factors which influence the incidence of compartment syndrome, ischaemic contracture, muscle necrosis and amputation. If blood flow to a limb cannot be restored early on then the incidence of these complications increases. The presence of severe concomitant injuries to veins, bone or soft tissue will increase this risk.

The effect of major vascular disruption is aggravated by hypovolaemic shock. Impaired tissue perfusion and a fall in tissue pO_2 increases capillary permeability. This results in an increased exudation of fluid into the interstitial space, which increases compartmental pressure causing venous pressure to rise leading to further exudation of fluid. With reduced blood flow there is widespread small vessel thrombosis. Muscle will tolerate ischaemia for four to eight hours, after which myonecrosis sets in (Scully and Hughes, 1956).

Even when circulation is restored promptly, the highly permeable capillary network may raise compartment pressures high enough to occlude large vessels. Shunting a major arterial injury at an early stage can restore circulation, limiting further ischaemic injury while other injuries are dealt with (Barros D'Sa and Moorehead, 1989).

The salvage rate in injured limbs falls sharply when long bone fractures accompany arterial injuries. In the past it was usual to repair the artery first. However, such vascular repair is susceptible to damage from long bone manipulation, bone fragments and traction (Connolly, 1970; O'Donnell et al, 1977).

Stabilising bone first minimises further tissue damage by bone fragments and prevents interruption of a vascular repair.

The practice of shunting arterial and venous injuries, allowing other injuries to be dealt with first, has favourably influenced the quality of surgical management, reducing complications and improving limb survival (Barros D'Sa, 1982; Elliot et al, 1984).

Fasciotomy

Compartment syndrome is seen after crushing or degloving injuries, especially when there is coexistent vascular injury. Untreated, it will lead to ischaemia and necrosis within that compartment. Fasciotomy should be carried out in any patient with undue pain in a limb, pain with passive motion or evidence of tightness in a compartment.

It is performed by incising the skin and deep fascia along the whole length of the affected area, decompressing the underlying tissues (Malsen et al, 1980).

Soft tissue infection

Traumatic wounds are particularly prone to invasive bacterial infection owing to the presence of devitalised tissue, foreign bodies and bacteria. Cellulitis is an infection superficial to the investing fascia of the skeletal musculature. In traumatic wounds it is often a rapidly spreading infection caused primarily by haemolytic streptococci. Treatment with penicillin is required.

Fasciitis is an infection of the fascial planes. Fascia is poorly suited for defence or localisation of infection. When severe wound oedema, pain and skin necrosis appear after injury, necrotising fasciitis should be considered. The skin appearance may belie the severity of the infection, which may only be signalled by a sudden fever, hypotension and confusion. Large amounts of extravascular fluid can be lost, and debridement of the area can require extensive excision of tissue.

Myositis represents a bacterial infection that has penetrated and destroyed muscle bundles. The most important post-traumatic form is clostridial in origin and represents the classic gas gangrene. It is rapidly disseminated within muscles and frequently requires both radical debridement and amputation.

Clostridial organisms are anaerobic, Gram-positive, spore-forming rods. When the spores are subject to anaerobic conditions they develop into toxin-producing bacteria.

An open wound is less likely to allow favourable anaerobic growth conditions. The recognition of myonecrosis is necessary for effective diagnosis and management. Such wounds are characterised by oedema and drainage of serosanguinous exudate. Exposure of the muscle bundles in these wounds will disclose intense swelling of the muscle with discoloration of the fibres. This ranges from salmon pink to a gangrenous greenish-blue colour. Typical crepitis may be palpable. The affected muscle will not contract on stimulation and may bleed if incised.

Systemic toxaemia will cause tachycardia, fever, disorientation and mild hypotension. Management requires correction of the fluid deficit, followed by full exposure and debridement of all tissues which may be infected.

Wound closure

The decision to close a wound is based on judgement and experience. When in doubt it is safer to leave a wound open and allow healing by secondary intention or close at a later stage by delayed primary suture (DPS).

If the traumatic wound is tidy, contamination is minimal and the time from injury to treatment is short, the wound can be cleaned and closed primarily with minimal infection risk.

If the wound is untidy then delayed closure is advised. Small untidy wounds with minimal tissue damage can be converted into tidy wounds by excision of the ragged wound edges and irrigation allowing primary closure. When suturing a wound it should be done without tension, leaving no dead space. The smallest size suture material practical for a wound should be used. Large contaminated wounds at risk of developing sepsis should be debrided, then left open and dressed. They can be closed by delayed primary suture or be left to heal by secondary intention. Plate 1 shows a severely infected sutured wound that should have been left open. Wounds unsuitable for DPS are covered with a split skin graft when clean.

Plate 1 shows a severely infected sutured wound that should have been left open.

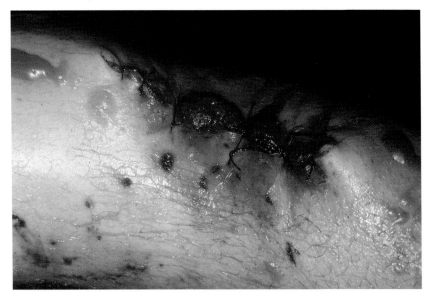

Plate 1 Infected sutured wound

Management of different traumatic wounds

Cuts and incisions

They are usually suitable for primary closure.

Stab wounds

The presence of underlying injury or contamination must be excluded. If tidy, they can be sutured primarily, otherwise debridement and delayed primary suture is necessary.

Shearing and degloving injuries

The commonest cause is the limb being trapped between the road and a moving vehicle tyre. Avulsion of the skin and subcutaneous tissues by a twisting mechanism ruptures the musculocutaneous and fasciocutaneous perforating vessels and devascularises the outer tissues.

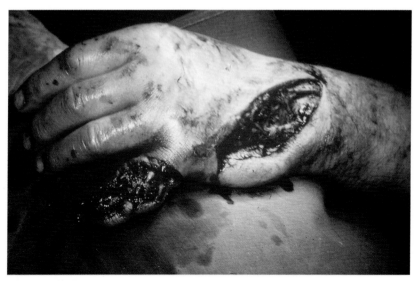

Plate 2 Degloving injury to hand

A degloving injury should be suspected if pallor, loss of sensation, friction burn, tyre imprint or abnormal skin mobility is present. Ischaemic skin is excised and the defect covered with a split skin graft. Harvesting the split skin graft from the degloved segment of skin is often possible. Primary reattachment of the skin by suture or compression usually fails.

Lower limb injuries

Until this century, wounds to the lower limbs with skin loss and damage to underlying tissues, especially bone, frequently resulted in amputation (Murry, 1990). In recent years the treatment of such injuries has changed dramatically and improved the outcome for patients (Byrd et al, 1981).

The use of external fracture stabilisation, radical debridement of devitalised soft tissue, second-look procedures and early muscle flap closure has reduced the incidence of complications such as non-union and infection.

Injuries from very high energy forces, which result in loss of large amounts of soft tissue and bone, remain a major problem. Success in managing these wounds is best achieved through an aggressive, collaborative effort between orthopaedic and plastic surgeons (Swartz and Mears, 1985).

In high-energy-induced trauma, the real soft tissue injury is usually far more extensive than initially appreciated (Byrd, 1981). All devitalised tissue, including devitalised bone, should be debrided before wound coverage is attempted. Serial debridement is often necessary as the extent of the injury becomes apparent. Gross defects resulting from adequate debridement require a large block of well-vascularised, undamaged tissue to cover a wound and obliterate dead space. Free muscle transfers provide this and are, therefore, reconstructive alternatives of choice.

Bone defects should be grafted as soon as possible after the soft tissue wound is closed and stable. Flap cover of lower limb skin defects is seldom needed. Split skin grafts are sufficient if there is a vascular recipient bed with no vital exposed structures.

The commonest cause of skin loss is the distally based, pretibial, traumatic skin flap, especially if it has been sutured back into place (Murry, 1990). This wound commonly occurs in elderly women and is notoriously difficult to treat as there is little subcutaneous tissue and poor blood supply. Excision of non-viable tissue and split skin grafting is usually required.

Missile injuries

Missile wounds represent a significant challenge for surgeons, who have to manage the great variety of injuries that can be inflicted. These wounds can cause widespread destruction to tissues and organs. Understanding the ballistics of the various missiles encountered is useful in predicting the amount of damage they may have caused.

The nature of a bullet wound depends largely on the velocity of that missile. The wounding power is directly proportional to the bullet's kinetic energy (Rich, 1980). This is determined by the formula $E = \frac{1}{2} mv^2$, where 'm' is the missile mass and 'v' its velocity. In the 20th century there has been a trend towards small, light missiles travelling at high velocities with very high kinetic energy, capable of causing massive injury.

There is no sharp cut-off point between high- and low-velocity bullets (Rich, 1980). A low-velocity bullet travels at around 200 metres per second, whereas a high-velocity bullet from a rifle travels at over 650 metres per second.

Any factor that will retard the bullet's forward and rotary speed will cause a more rapid release of energy. Such factors are tissue density, the bluntness of the point of the bullet, its yaw and the degree of tumbling as it travels through tissue.

In low-velocity bullet wounds, such as those caused by most handguns, the main injury is caused by the transit of the bullet through the tissues, and damage is slight unless important structures are traversed. Penetrating bullets crush and lacerate the tissues in their immediate path but at low velocity do not cause damage beyond the tract.

The entrance wound is circular and smaller than the bullet's diameter, owing to tissue resilience at the point of entrance. The exit wound is usually a ragged slit or star shape owing to the tumbling of the bullet as it passes through the soft tissues. If the gun was fired from close range there will be characteristic powder burns around the entrance wound. Treatment of low-velocity wounds will depend on the damage caused. If it is limited to soft tissue, minimal debridement may be all that is required.

High-velocity bullet wounds present a much greater challenge. They cause a temporary cavitation effect (Cooper and Ryan, 1990) which can be 30 times the size of the residual tract of the bullet. This is due to the retardation effect of tissues, causing a sudden release of an enormous amount of energy.

The higher the velocity, the greater the cavity produced. The cavitation effect causes widespread tissue damage and in muscle results in an area of bloody, pulpy or dead tissue owing to rupture of capillaries between the muscle fibres. There will also be damage to adjacent structures which may not be immediately apparent at the time of initial debridement.

Thrombosis to blood vessels and injury to stretched nerves occurs. Long bones can be fractured even though not struck directly. The tissues are unable to contain the force of the temporary cavitation and an explosive exit wound is produced. The difference in injury pattern between high- and low-velocity bullets is illustrated in Figure 1.

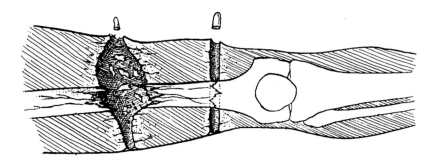

Figure 1 High- and low-velocity bullet injuries

The same general principles of wound management apply. Wounds must be explored thoroughly and one should err on the side of a more radical excision (Marcus et al, 1961).

The skin and subcutaneous tissues should be incised generously to get to the depths of the wound. Deep fascia must be incised along the length of the incision, as this allows good exposure to the depths of the wound. Dead muscle, fat and fascia is excised along with dirt, debris, missiles and blood clot. Small metal fragments can be difficult to find, and prolonged exploratory surgery is unnecessary. The foreign materials that must be removed because of their tendency to cause severe wound infection are dirt, cloth and extrinsic bone fragments.

Bomb blast injuries

Exposure to explosive blast results in a well-documented pattern of injury (Hull, 1992; Hadden et al, 1978).The components that cause injury are, first, the shockwave, with its sharp leading edge of almost instantaneous pressure rise from ambient air pressure, to the over-pressure created by the explosion, known as the shock front. This lasts a few milliseconds and is followed by a negative phase of low pressure of longer duration. Second, the dynamic overpressure, or blast wind, is the mass movement of the gaseous products of detonation away from the point of the explosion.

The shockwave is responsible for the primary blast injury, blast lung and tympanic membrane rupture. The dynamic overpressure causes secondary injury from objects caught in the blast wave, such as grit, stones, metal, masonry and glass (Plate 3).

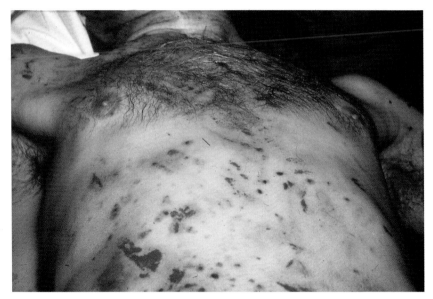

Plate 3 Bomb blast injury

These fragments can travel at over 2,000 metres/sec, acting as high velocity missiles, producing severe tissue injury. The most frequent cause of injury in bomb blasts is due to these secondary missiles (Hull, 1992). Victims may also be injured by indirect violence as they are flung against surrounding objects. The vulnerability of the head and neck is emphasised by the fact that brain damage and skull fracture are commonly seen in the fatally wounded. Diffuse lung contusions, eardrum rupture and liver laceration are also commonly seen, along with serious soft tissue damage. Plate 4 illustrates traumatic lower limb dismemberment following blast injury.

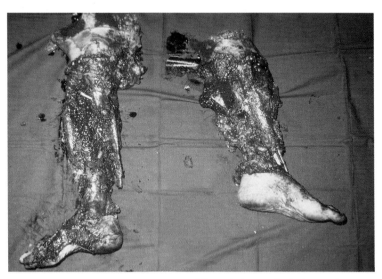

Plate 4 Lower limb dismemberment

All wounds must be explored, no matter how trivial they seem on initial inspection. Primary amputation of injured limbs is often required. Thorough debridement is necessary as there will be gross tissue damage and contamination.

Conclusion

The variety of traumatic wounds encountered is enormous. They vary from small, clean incisions to grossly contaminated, multiple tissue injuries which can be life-threatening. The basic principles of wound management apply in every case. The importance of adequate wound debridement and exploration to exclude underlying injury must not be overlooked.

References

Barros D'Sa, A.A.B. (1982) A decade of missile induced vascular trauma. *Annals of the Royal College of Surgeons of England*; 64: 1, 37–44.

Barros D'Sa, A.A.B., Moorehead, R.J. (1989) Combined arterial and venous intraluminal shunting in major trauma of the lower limb. *European Journal of Vascular Surgery*; 3: 6, 577–581.

Byrd, H.S. et al (1981) The management of open tibial fractures with associated soft tissue loss: external pin fixation with early flap coverage. *Plastic and Reconstructive Surgery*; 68: 1, 73–82.

Cooper, G.J., Ryan, J.M. (1990) Interaction of penetrating missiles with tissues: some common misapprensions and implications for wound management. *British Journal of Surgery*; 77: 6, 606–610.

Connolly, J. (1970) Management of fractures associated with arterial injuries. *American Journal of Surgery*; 120: 3, 331–334.

Elliot, J. et al (1984) Combined bony and vascular limb trauma: a new approach to treatment. *Journal of Bone and Joint Surgery*; 66B: 2, 281.

Hadden, W.A. et al (1978) The injuries of terrorist bombing: a study of 1,532 consecutive patients. *British Journal of Surgery*; 65: 8, 525–531.

Haury, B. et al (1978) Debridement: an essential component of traumatic wound care. *American Journal of Surgery*; 135: 2, 238–242.

Hull, J.B. (1992) Traumatic amputation by explosive blast: pattern of injury in survivors. *British Journal of Surgery*; 79: 12, 1303–1306.

McNicholl, B.P. et al (1992) Subclinical injuries in lacerations to the forearm and hand. *British Journal of Surgery*; 79: 8, 765–767.

Malsen, F.A. et al (1980) Diagnosis and management of compartmental syndromes. *Journal of Bone and Joint Surgery* (US edition); 62: 2, 286–291.

Marcus, N.A. et al (1961) Low velocity gunshot wounds to the extremities. *Journal of Trauma*; 1: 4, 354–360.

Murry, D.S. (1990) Skin loss of the lower limb. *Injury*; 21: 5, 309–310.

O'Donnell, T.F. et al (1977) Arterial injuries associated with fractures and/or dislocations of the knee. *Journal of Trauma*; 17: 10, 341–344.

Rich, N.M. (1980) Missile injuries. *American Journal of Surgery*; 139: 3, 414–420.

Rosen, J.S., Cleary, J.E. (1991) Surgical management of wounds. *Clinics in Podiatric Medicine and Surgery*; 8: 4, 891–907.

Scully, R.W., Hughes, C.W. (1956) Pathology of ischaemia of skeletal muscle in man. *American Journal of Pathology*; 32: 805–829.

Swartz, W.M., Mears, D.C. (1985) The role of free tissue transfer in lower-extremity reconstruction. *Plastic and Reconstructive Surgery*; 76: 3, 364–373.

5 Burns

Ann Fowler

Key points

▶ An accurate history is essential in determining the extent of the trauma and to facilitate treatment

▶ Burns are classified according to cause, extent (surface area burnt), depth and history of injury

▶ The aim of treatment is to provide comfort, emotional care, infection control and wound care

Introduction

Successful management of burns depends on the nurse's knowledge and skill in assessment, wound care, infection control, pain relief, ability to provide emotional support and ability to obtain specialist input as appropriate. The ultimate goal for all burn patients is successful reintegration into their home, school or work and community.

Initial management

Before considering the burn itself, the 'ABC' of trauma management (airway, breathing, circulation) should be implemented, followed by a more detailed assessment of the burn injury and the patient (Dimick and Rue, 1988). Burns are classified according to cause, extent, depth and history of the injury. These, along with the potential for respiratory problems or other traumatic injuries, will establish the severity of injury.

Burn assessment

The causes of injury can be classified as accidental, non-accidental or attempted suicide. Various physical and emotional conditions or disorders such as epilepsy, alcohol, drugs or depression can predispose an individual to burn injury (Darko et al, 1986; Lawrence, 1996).

Obtaining an accurate history is essential in determining the extent of trauma and facilitating optimal treatment. If there are any suspicions or concerns regarding breathing difficulties or inhalation of steam, smoke or gases, the patient must be referred immediately for medical review in a hospital setting.

Burn injuries can occur from dry heat such as flame, contact injuries, scalds or chemical and electrical burns. Radiation accidents are rare with the exception of ultra-violet light. Scald injuries in adults usually cause partial thickness burns but in children or elderly people can cause full thickness burns. Hot oil can cause more serious depth burns owing to the higher temperature and prolonged contact. Small electrical or chemical injuries, classified as minor burns, should be reviewed by a specialist unit as they may require excision and grafting (Table 1).

Burn	Common examples
Dry heat	Domestic, industrial or road traffic accidents involving flash, flame, contact or friction; that is, house fires, bonfires, barbecues, bitumen, car accidents
Wet heat (scalds)	Domestic or industrial accidents involving bath water, showers, steam, hot drinks, hot oil
Chemical:	
acid	Industrial accidents involving hydrochloric, sulphuric or hydrofluoric acid
alkaline	Domestic accidents involving sodium hydroxide (caustic soda), potassium hydroxide (alkaline batteries), ammonia, cement
Electrical:	
low voltage	Domestic accidents involving flash or direct contact with <1,000 volts
high voltage	Industrial accidents involving construction work or power lines involving flash or 'true' high tension electrical injury (direct contact or arc) with >1,000 volts
Radiation	Accidental exposure to ultra-violet light (sun lamps/direct sun), X-rays and gamma rays
Intense cold	Industrial accidents involving contact with liquid oxygen, liquid nitrogen or extremely cold metals

Table 1 Types and causes of burn injuries

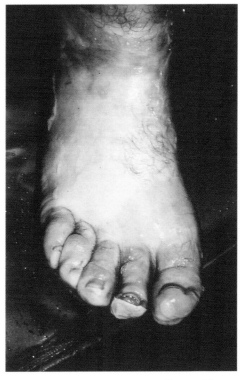

Chemical burn

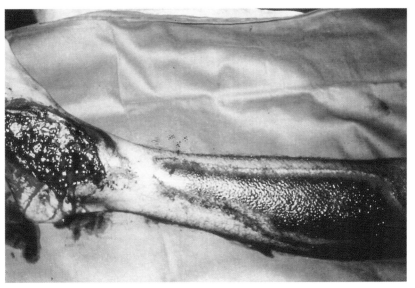

Electrical burn

Extent of burn (burn surface area)

The extent of a burn is described by a percentage that indicates the amount of the total body surface area (TBSA) involved. The Rule of Nines (Figure 1) allows for a gross estimate for adult patients but in children the Lund and Browder chart (Figure 2) allows for a more accurate assessment. A less refined method of calculating surface loss is to use the palm of the patient's hand, with fingers closed: this approximates to 1% TBSA.

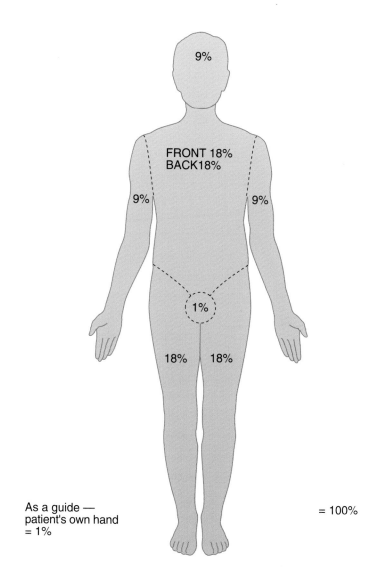

Figure 1 The Rule of Nines

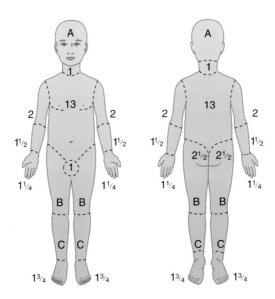

Figure 2 The Lund and Browder paediatric assessment chart

Relative percentages affected by growth						
Area	Age 0	1	5	10	15	Adult
A = half of head	$9\frac{1}{2}$	$8\frac{1}{2}$	$6\frac{1}{2}$	$5\frac{1}{2}$	$4\frac{1}{2}$	$3\frac{1}{2}$
B = half of one thigh	$2\frac{3}{4}$	$3\frac{1}{4}$	4	$4\frac{1}{4}$	$4\frac{1}{2}$	$4\frac{3}{4}$
C = half of one leg	$2\frac{1}{2}$	$2\frac{1}{2}$	$2\frac{3}{4}$	3	$3\frac{1}{4}$	$3\frac{1}{2}$

Table 2 Relative percentages affected by growth

Assessing surface loss is crucial to identifying patients who need to be hospitalised and receive intravenous fluid replacement therapy. Those patients at risk of hypovolaemic shock are adults with burns of 15% TBSA or more and children with burns of 10% TBSA or more. Other less critical burns may be treated simply with extra oral administration of fluids (Muir et al, 1987).

These are only guidelines, and patients with burns of a smaller TBSA may still need hospitalising because of physiological, emotional, medical or psycho-social needs.

Classification of depth

The depth of tissue penetrated by the thermal insult determines classification. The various severities are defined as:

▶ superficial
▶ superficial-partial
▶ deep-partial (deep dermal)
▶ full thickness

Wound characteristics and healing potential are summarised in Table 3.

Depth of burn	Skin structures involved	Key characteristics	Scar formation
Superficial	Epidermis	Skin dry and intact, red, very painful, blanches under pressure Minimal tissue damage, may form blisters up to 48 hours after initial injury	Heals well within 3–7 days with minimal or no treatment No obvious scarring
Superficial-partial thickness	Epidermis and superficial dermis	Blisters immediately, red in areas, moist and exuding, brisk capillary refill (blanches under pressure), very painful (sensitive to air and temperature)	Should heal within 10–21 days if no infection or pressure within or on the wound May appear very red for approximately first six weeks, then hypo-pigmented or hyper-pigmented depending on amount of remaining intact melanocytes
Deep-partial thickness (deep dermal)	Epidermis and dermis Hair follicles and sebaceous glands intact	White/creamy in colour, large easily 'liftable' blisters Slightly painful with areas that are insensate	Will take >30 days to heal and therefore preferable to skin graft early to maximise healing and scar formation
Full thickness	Epidermis and dermis Subcutaneous tissue and/or deeper structures if chemical or electrical injury	May appear waxy white, cherry red, grey or leathery in appearance Minimal or no pain in actual wound No response to temperature or pressure No capillary refill	Requires skin grafting as few regenerative elements remain in skin structure to allow for spontaneous healing Scar will be influenced by genetic predisposition and grafting techniques

Table 3 Defining burn depth

It is often difficult to distinguish the exact depth of burn in the first few days, and many burns are 'mixed' in depth. All patients should be reviewed between 48 and 72 hours after injury, and follow-up should continue until the wound is fully re-epithelialised. Regardless of the initial assessment of depth, the patient should always be informed of the potential need for skin grafting and the scarring expected.

What is a minor burn?

It has been suggested that there are approximately 13,000 patients a year in the UK who require hospitalisation for burn and scald injuries (Lawrence, 1996). There are various definitions of what constitutes a minor burn or scald injury and what type of burns can be managed on an out-patient basis, but one commonly used classification for minor burns is 'a partial thickness burn involving less than 5% body surface area in adults… any burn not anticipated to require a skin graft' (Gower, 1996).

Classifying a burn as 'minor' may suggest that it does not require specialist expertise, should heal with the minimum of interference and does not require hospitalisation, but this type of injury should never be dismissed as insignificant (Marsden, 1996).

Major burns

Patients identified as having a major burn or an inhalation injury should be admitted to a burns unit. Patients not suitable for home care or outpatient management are identified in Table 4.

Type or % of burn	Rationale
Indeterminate depth burns of the face	Risk of peri-orbital oedema, possible airway difficulties and poor cosmetic appearance for the patient
Burns involving the eye(s)	Risk of corneal abrasion or other ophthalmic complications Should be examined and reviewed by ophthalmologist
Partial to deep dermal thickness burns involving the hand(s)	Self-care at home is very difficult and skin grafting may be required
Partial or deep thickness burns involving the lower extremities and/or the feet	Restriction in mobilisation and risk of oedema in dependent lower extremity could convert partial thickness burn into full thickness injury
Burns of the perineum or buttocks	Difficulties with mobilisation, hygiene and appropriate wound care measures
Patients who have self-inflicted burn wounds or attempted suicide	Reduce risk of further self-harm or death by giving patient full mental health assessment
Children or elderly people with minor burns requiring additional medical or social support	Reduce risk of further injury by identifying and solving initial cause of burn or scald Maintain the patient's safety and well-being
Well-defined burns on any part of the body which can be excised and grafted early (same day or up to first seven days post-injury)	Reduce the severity and outcome of injury through early surgery Reduce the risk of local/systemic infection, inadequate pain relief, poor wound healing and scar maturation

Table 4 Patients not suitable for home care or out-patient management

Patient assessment

Assessment may take place in a hospital, primary care setting or the patient's own home. In addition to classification of burn surface area and depth, other factors have to be considered when determining whether a patient can be managed on an out-patient basis:

► location of burn(s)

► age

► general medical status

► home care situation; family, friends and community support

► motivation and coping skills.

The area affected may indicate whether the patient can meet all the activities of daily living, including work or school. Patients with hand burns may require hospitalisation for analgesia, elevation and physiotherapy; those with facial burns or perineal burns may require daily dressings and constant supervision. This may not be practical at home.

The age of the patient will also influence progress and outcome. Young children with 'borderline' burns (5–10% TBSA) may require hospitalisation to provide parental or family support. Elderly or infirm patients may require admission and/or stabilisation of other medical conditions. Patients with pre-existing cardiac, renal or pulmonary conditions are at greater risk of exacerbation of their original disorder or delayed wound healing (Turner, 1998).

Questioning about the patient's social and emotional status can provide indications as to whether they can manage, as opposed to contend with, difficulties at home. Some of the issues to consider include:

▶ patient's ability to keep wound clean and manage own dressing

▶ patient's ability to recognise complications

▶ patient's ability to act on information given

▶ patient's ability to learn and perform care required

▶ patient's ability to return regularly for review (if required)

▶ potential social problems/issues arising from incident

▶ previous medical history/coping skills

Keeping the patient informed of their progress and giving them realistic timescales for healing and resuming normal activities should lessen their anxiety, encourage their trust in the nurse, and increase co-operation with dressings and exercise regimes.

Treatment plan

This should include the provision of comfort, information, infection control and wound care. It is important to inform and discuss the care plan with the patient, including the need for:

▶ good fluid and nutritional intake, as a high-calorie and high-protein diet is essential for burn wound healing (Gottschlich and Jenkins, 1998)

▶ exercise, maintaining a full range of movement, and the possible use of splints (some partial or deep dermal wounds may require additional support to maintain appropriate positioning and movement)

▶ good personal and oral hygiene

▶ protection of the wound from external moisture or trauma

Tetanus prophylaxis is required even for minor wounds (Lindsey, 1984). Where anti-bacterial cover is required, silver sulphadiazine is a proven agent against pseudomonal and staphylococcal infections (Konop, 1991). Oral or intravenous antibiotics should be administered where appropriate and as prescribed.

Burn wound care

The aim of wound care in burns is to:

► maintain a clean, moist wound environment

► promote patient comfort

► offer protection from infection or further trauma

► facilitate optimal activity and function

Burn care begins with the initial first aid measure of applying cool water for 10–20 minutes. The only exceptions to this rule are electrical injuries, facial burns and burns involving certain chemical agents (metallic sodium, potassium and calcium react violently with aqueous solutions). Water will cool the area, reduce tissue damage and relieve pain (Lawrence, 1987). Subsequent dressing changes should involve cleaning the wound with warmed tap water, warmed sterile saline or sterile water (depending on local wound care policies) and a non-perfumed bland soap, as removal of loose or devitalised tissue is essential to reduce the risk of infection. Cleaning is discontinued once granulation tissue is present.

Treating blisters on partial thickness wounds remains controversial. Studies exist to support draining blister fluid, initially leaving the roof of the blister intact as a biological dressing, and then debriding the blister at the next change of dressing (Rockwell and Ehrlich, 1990; Garner et al, 1993). Others have suggested that, when clinically appropriate, the burn blister is a suitable dressing for the burn wound (Hartford, 1996). Where it is not practical to leave the blister intact, the use of an occlusive or semi-permeable dressing over a clean healing wound maintains the wound in its own exudate (Wilson et al, 1994).

Wound swabbing for microbiological surveillance is not required immediately after the injury, nor is it necessary routinely to swab a minor burn unless the patient shows symptoms of an infection (Turner, 1998).

Dressings

The choice of dressing should be based on the characteristics of the dressing (Turner, 1982), burn depth, area, site, patient acceptability, cost and ease of use. The choice of dressings and selection relevant for superficial and partial thickness burns are identified in Table 5.

Dressing	Advantages	Disadvantages
Group 1 Paraffin gauze	Allows passage of exudate into external dressing pad Less expensive option for first 48–72 hours as review essential in first few days	Not waterproof, have no absorbent capabilities Needs frequent changes as can stick to the wound, causing pain on removal Needs a secondary dressing
Group 2 Low-adherent dressings	Do not adhere to wound surface Not painful to apply or remove (Other advantages as for Group 1)	May move/fall off wound surface Need a secondary dressing
Group 3 Hydrocolloids	Virtually impermeable to water vapour Good barrier properties to infection Can be left *in situ* for 5–7 days	May change appearance of wound On removal the smell may be offensive Not suitable on burn surface areas larger than 10% TBSA Adhesive properties of some products may cause pain on removal Cannot easily view the wound surface (need to ensure patient is reviewed at regular intervals)
Group 4 Hydrogels	Rehydrate dry or dead tissue Can be used at most stages of healing Comfortable to apply and may be soothing to patien	Require a secondary dressing
Group 5 Vapour-permeable adhesive film	Provides a moist healing environment Useful for shallow, flat surface wounds Can be used as secondary dressings with hydrogels	Cannot absorb exudate Not ideal for infected wounds Require skill and attention for application in practice Patient may not wish to view their wounds
Group 6 Polyurethane foam/hydropolymers	Absorbs fluid May be waterproof Provides thermal insulation Comfortable for patient	Adhesive properties of some products may cause pain on removal Cannot easily view the wound surface so need to ensure patient is reviewed at regular intervals

Table 5 Examples of choice and selection of dressings for superficial and partial thickness burns

Hand burns

Hand burns involving three fingers or fewer can be dressed individually with finger 'bobs'. Larger areas on the hand can be successfully managed in plastic or polythene bags (Slater and Hughes, 1971), together with an antibacterial cream. These dressings need at least daily changes. Reassessment and documentation of the size and depth of the burn is essential at each dressing review.

Scars

Initially scars from the burn site may appear red or purple changing to a paler white, beige or pink colour. These colour changes are quite obvious and may be more apparent with changes in environment temperature. Aftercare information specific to the patient's scars should be provided by the referring specialist centre.

Significant resolution of excess scar tissue cannot be expected in less than a year, and remodelling of collagen can take up to five years (Haynes, 1981). The nurse should be able to act as a sympathetic listener and give advice and support regarding aftercare and expected outcomes, although specialised support or counselling may be needed for more traumatised or emotionally distressed patients.

Follow-up for patients with wounds and dressings

Specific instructions for the patient regarding their burn wound should be clear and comprehensible (Fitzpatrick et al, 1985). The information should include:

▶ basic guidelines for wound management

▶ expected events during the healing phase

▶ the need to elevate the injured area (if applicable)

▶ date of review (within 48–72 hours after the first assessment)

▶ appropriate use of pain medication

▶ the need to contact the GP/hospital if the patient has a fever or feels unwell

▶ 24-hour contact numbers for events that may require immediate care

Physical and emotional aftercare

Healed areas can be massaged regularly with moisturising oils or creams of the patient's choice to provide lubrication and relieve the discomfort of itching (Mertens et al, 1997). Oils containing nuts should be used with caution in children or those with known allergic reactions. The healed wound may be sensitive to sunlight, so a high-factor sunscreen is recommended for the first year. This can be decreased thereafter.

Burn patients can have disturbed sleep because of the injury itself or because pain and discomfort may interfere with the normal circadian rhythm (Blakeney and Meyer, 1994). Anti-pruritic agents prescribed for itching may help if increased at night-time to induce drowsiness, or a short course of sedation can be prescribed.

Both the patient and family require support to accept the injury and its impact. Regardless of the severity of the injury, most patients have significant concerns about the appearance of their wound after healing and questions about whether the scar can be improved by surgery (Haynes, 1981).

Conclusion

A systematic and organised plan of care will provide burn patients with optimum treatment. The nurse should be able to identify potential complications for patients with acute minor burn injuries, whether they are treated as an out-patient from a regional burns unit or are managed in the community setting. The overall goals are to facilitate healing physically and emotionally, minimise the risk of infection, and return the patient to a productive and normal environment according to their lifestyle.

References

Blakeney, P.E., Meyer, W.J. (1994) Psycho-social aspects of burn care. *Trauma Quarterly*; 2: 2, 166–179.

Darko, D.F. et al (1986) Analysis of 585 burn patients hospitalised over a six-year period. Part III: psychosocial data. *Burns*; 12: 384–390.

Dimick, A.R., Rue, L.W. (1988) Outpatient treatment of burns. *Alabama Journal of Medical Sciences*; 25: 2, 183–186.

Fitzpatrick, K.T. et al (1985) Outpatient management of minor burns. *Physician Assistant*; 9: 5–28.

Garner, W.L. et al (1993) The effects of burn blister fluid on keratinocyte replication and differentiation. *Journal of Burn Care and Rehabilitation*; 14: 127–131.

Gottschlich, M.M., Jenkins, M.E. (1998) Metabolic consequences and nutritional needs. In: Carrougher, G.J. *Burn Care and Therapy*. St Louis: C.V. Mosby.

Gower, J. (1996) *Report of the Burns Working Group*. London: North and South Thames NHS Regions.

Hartford, C.E. (1996) Care of outpatient burns In: Herndon, D.N. (ed.) *Total Burn Care*. Philadelphia: W.B. Saunders.

Haynes, B.W. (1981) Emergency department management of minor burns. *Topics in Emergency Medicine*; 3: 35–40.

Konop, D.J. (1991) General local treatment. In: Trofino, R.B. *Nursing Care of the Burn Injured Patient*. Philadelphia: F.A. Davies.

Lawrence, J.C. (1987) British Burn Association recommended first aid for burns and scalds. *Burns*; 13: 2, 153.

Lawrence, J.C. (1996) Burns and scalds: aetiology and prevention. In: Settle, J.A.D. (ed.) *Principles and Practice of Burns Management*. London: Churchill Livingstone.

Lindsey, D. (1984) Tetanus prophylaxis: do our guidelines assure protection? *Journal of Trauma*; 24: 1063–1064.

Marsden, A.K. (1996) Minor burns. In: Settle, J.A.D. (ed.) *Principles and Practice of Burns Management*. London: Churchill Livingstone.

Mertens, D.M. et al (1997) Outpatient burn management. *Nursing Clinics of North America*; 32: 2, 343–364.

Muir, I.F.K. et al (1987) *Burns and Their Treatment* (third edition). London: Butterworth.

Rockwell, W.B., Ehrlich, H.P. (1990) Should burn blister fluid be evacuated? *Journal of Burn Care and Rehabilitation*; 11: 93–95.

Slater, R.M., Hughes, N.C. (1971) A simplified method of treating burns of the hand. *British Journal of Plastic Surgery*; 24: 296.

Turner, T.D. (1982) Which dressing and why? *Nursing Times* (supplement); 78: 29, 1–5.

Turner, D.G. (1998) Ambulatory care of the burn patient. In: Carrougher, G.J. *Burn Care and Therapy*. St Louis: C.V. Mosby.

Wilson, Y. et al (1994) Investigation of the presence and role of calmodulin and other mitogens in human burn blister fluid. *Journal of Burn Care and Rehabilitation*; 15: 303–314.

6 Venous leg ulceration

Mark Collier

Key points

▶ Leg ulceration affects approximately 1% of the adult population in the UK

▶ A differential diagnosis must be made before assessing the wound

▶ Therapy to counteract the effects of venous hypertension is used in conjunction with wound management strategies

Epidemiology

Leg ulceration, defined as 'a loss of skin below the knee on the leg or foot which takes more than six weeks to heal' (Dale and Callam, 1983), has been reported as affecting approximately 1% of the adult population in the UK (Laing, 1992). In general terms, this means that at any one time almost 100,000 patients will have an open ulcer requiring professional intervention and a further 400,000 will have a healed ulcer which is likely to recur (Callam et al, 1985). The resultant workload for health care professionals in acute or community settings is high, and the associated costs to the NHS have been estimated at between £300m and £600m a year (Bosanquet, 1992; Bosanquet et al, 1993).

Perhaps more importantly, recent research has begun to identify the considerable suffering patients with a chronic leg ulcer endure. In particular, effects on their quality of life have been analysed in order to validate these as an outcome indicator (Franks et al, 1994; Franks, 1998).

Venous ulceration is the major cause of leg ulcers, comprising 70–75% of the total, with the remaining 25–30% mostly consisting of arterial, neuropathic and mixed aetiology ulcers. A small percentage are caused by more unusual pathophysiologies (see Box 1) (Cornwall et al, 1986; Cameron, 1992; Collier, 1996a).

▶ vascular disease

▶ haematological disease

▶ metabolic disease

▶ trauma

▶ wound infection

▶ systemic infection

▶ neoplasms

▶ mixed aetiology

Box I Causes of chronic leg ulceration

To ensure appropriate treatment is provided it is vital for an experienced professional to identify a differential diagnosis before assessing the wound. Assessment of the whole patient, not just their ulcer, is essential (Collier, 1994; Miller and Dyson, 1996). It is also important that staff caring for patients with venous leg ulceration have a sound knowledge of the relevant anatomy. This is essential to understand visible signs and symptoms that may be related to the ulcer.

Venous ulceration: relevant anatomy

The role of the vascular (circulatory) system (Figure 1) is to circulate blood around the body in order to provide oxygen and other nutrients to body tissues, while also assisting with the removal of toxins and other waste products. Veins are blood vessels that convey deoxygenated blood from the tissues back to the heart.

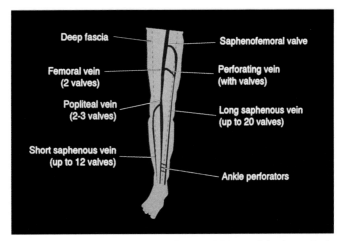

Figure I Veins of the lower limb

Veins are similar in anatomical structure to arteries, both comprising three main layers: the tunica intima; tunica media; and tunica adventitia, also known as externa (Tortora and Anagnostakos, 1987).

The tunica intima is the inner layer of the tube-like structure and is made up of single layers of epithelium and some connective tissue. The tunica media consists mainly of smooth muscle and elastic-type tissue. The tunica adventitia is composed of fibrous connective tissue, fibroblasts and mature collagen fibres. These layers, while consistent throughout the vascular system, vary in thickness regionally depending on the function of the particular vessel.

The wall of a vein is thinner and less muscular than that of an artery. Nevertheless, veins have the ability to dilate and accommodate as much as 80% of an individual's total circulating volume if required (Dale, 1995).

Small subdivisions of veins that connect to the capillary network (microcirculation) are known as venules and their function is simply to drain blood from the capillaries to the veins.

Other important features of the venous system, relevant to ulcer development, are that:

► unlike arteries, veins have valves which normally allow blood to flow only in one direction (Figure 2)

► venous return of blood from the lower limbs is assisted by the calf muscle which acts as a pump; venous return can be affected by gravity and posture

► varicose veins damage the valves and, in turn, cause a backflow of blood resulting in raised pressure in the superficial veins (Moffatt and Harper, 1997)

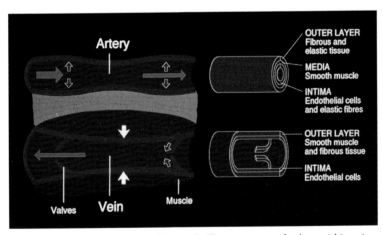

Figure 2 The structure of valves within veins

The venous system of the lower limb consists of both superficial and deep veins, with veins known as perforators connecting the two. Normally blood flows from the superficial to the deep veins via the perforators.

The superficial veins (the great and small saphenous veins) are designed to carry blood back to the heart under low pressure, whereas the deep veins (posterior and anterior tibial, popliteal and femoral veins) are designed to carry blood back to the heart under higher pressure. The perforators connect the superficial and deep systems and pass through the fascia and other structures of the lower limb.

Damage to the veins (for example, as the result of a deep vein thrombosis) results in either a loss of function or destruction of the valves, leading to a rise of pressure in smaller vessels. This is often referred to as venous hypertension and can be defined as an excessive pressure within the veins and capillaries resulting from damage to any part of the venous system.

Normally, a pressure balance is maintained on either side of the capillary wall by hydrostatic pressure, osmotic pressure and the properties of the vessel walls (Hinchliff and Montague, 1988). But when venous hypertension goes unchecked, the associated vessel walls become distorted and more permeable, allowing larger molecules to pass from the intra- to the extra-vascular spaces. The end result can be a venous leg ulcer. Oedema is often associated with venous leg ulceration and is a direct result of the above mechanisms.

Clinical signs of venous hypertension

Prolonged venous hypertension produced a number of effects that may be noticed by practitioners:

Varicose veins   a sign of chronic venous hypertension resulting from damage to valves in the lower limb veins. These can be identified in approximately 20% of the population (Stemmer, 1969) and people with occupations that involve periods of prolonged standing, particularly in warm environments, are particularly at risk

Ankle flare   a distinctive vein pattern noted on the medial (inner) aspect of the ankle as a result of distension of the veins in that region

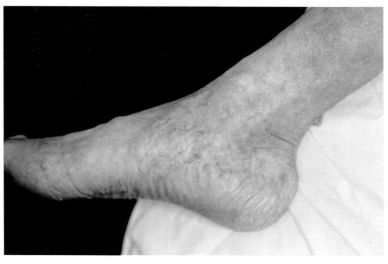

Ankle flare

Lipodermatosclerosis a change in the texture of the skin (induration) as fat is replaced by fibrous tissue. Often the affected leg resembles an inverted champagne bottle

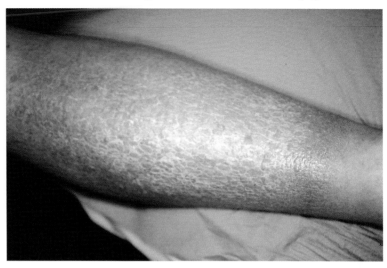

Lipodermatosclerosis

Skin staining a red/brown pigmentation of the surrounding tissues occurs when haemosiderin (a breakdown product of haemoglobin) is released owing to distension of the vessel walls and leakage of red blood cells into the interstitial fluid/space. This staining is sometimes included under the term lipodermatosclerosis. It can be chronic or acute and may be confused with infection in the acute phase

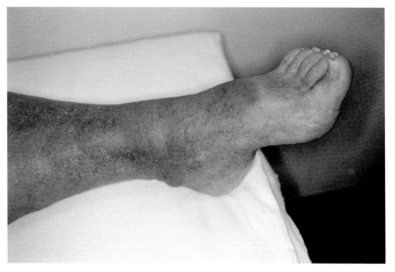

Lipodermatosclerosis (staining)

Skin atrophy	the dermis becomes thin as a result of a reduced blood supply, making it particularly susceptible to local trauma
Eczema	skin changes of an eczematous nature are often associated with venous insufficiency. The reaction may be described as wet or dry, localised or general in nature

Assessing patients with a venous ulcer

The principles underpinning assessment of patients presenting with a venous ulcer have discussed in detail elsewhere (Hinchliff and Montague, 1988; Morison et al, 1998) but can be summarised as follows:

▶ identify the underlying aetiology – venous, arterial or other

▶ identify any factors local to the ulcer or specific to the patient's lifestyle, for example, smoking, which may delay healing

▶ identify any current medical conditions or interventions which may affect healing

▶ identify the most appropriate treatment regime

▶ identify the optimum health care environment

Specific indications that an ulcer is venous are shown in Table 1.

Site of ulcer	Usually seen around the area of the medial malleolus
Appearance/size of ulcer	Usually superficial, irregular in shape but extensive in total surface area
Associated exudate production	High exudate production is common
Oedema	Tends to be generalised, reduces with leg elevation
Colour of surrounding skin	Characteristic brown staining often noted
Presence of any varicosities	Patient often has a history of varicose veins or evidence of ankle flare
Pain history	Generally reported as a dull ache, relieved by elevation of the affected limb
Nature of foot pulses	Generally unaffected, strong and palpable

Table 1 Specific indications of a venous ulcer

Although the signs in Table 1 are clearly indicative of venous disease, it is important that a differential diagnosis is not made solely on clinical signs. Ideally a full vascular assessment, involving evaluation of arterial, venous and lymphatic circulation, should be undertaken to confirm the diagnosis of an ulcer or to assist with ongoing assessment and re-evaluation. Hand-held Doppler ultrasound machines are often used to assist with this process, but these will only assess the arterial component.

Doppler ultrasound assessment

This technique (Moffatt and Harper, 1997; Vowden et al, 1996) involves recording systolic pressure with a hand-held ultrasound Doppler at the foot or ankle (A) usually taken at the dorsalis pedis or posterior tibial pulse and brachial artery (B). A is then divided by B to obtain a ratio. This is referred to as the ankle brachial pressure index (ABPI) or resting pressure index (RPI).

Generally, a result of 0.8 or higher indicates that it is safe to apply compression, although some specialist centres compress at lower ratios. A normal reading will be around 1; higher readings might indicate arterial calcification. The presence of palpable foot pulses does not exclude significant arterial disease (Moffatt and O'Hare, 1995a). It is important that Doppler ultrasound assessment is undertaken by suitably trained and experienced professionals. In addition, the ratio should not be seen as absolute.

Managing patients with a venous ulcer

Once a differential diagnosis of the ulcer is confirmed and an assessment completed and recorded, the task is to optimise the patient's healing potential (Collier, 1996b). This can be achieved by maintaining the ideal local wound environment and therapy to counteract the effects of venous hypertension.

General assessment and management principles relevant to the local wound environment have been discussed in detail elsewhere (Moffatt and Harper, 1997; Morison et al, 1998; Flanagan, 1997) and are summarised as follows:

▶ identify if the wound bed and/or surrounding skin needs cleaning and, if so, with what solution

▶ grade the wound with the aid of a colour or numerical grading tool (or both) and identify whether the wound requires debridement (Collier, 1994). If so, decide which is the most appropriate method (Bale, 1997)

▶ record the surface area of the wound using either a ruler, clear acetate tracing/wound lesion measure, photography, computer software or a combination of these methods

▶ establish whether or not the wound is infected and, if so, identify the appropriate treatment regime

▶ identify treatment objectives for management of the wound and select the most appropriate dressing material(s) to achieve this (Collier, 1994)

▶ consider the state of the skin surrounding the ulcer. Apply topical medications as prescribed, if clinically indicated (for eczema, for example), or protective agents (barrier creams) to reduce the risk of skin maceration, and/or topical emollients to reduce the effects of skin dehydration

Compression therapy: the key to countering the effects of venous hypertension

A number of studies have confirmed the effectiveness of graduated compression of the lower limb (40mmHg at the ankle reducing to 17mmHg just below the knee) in improving venous function (Stemmer, 1969; Gaylarde et al, 1993; Moffatt, 1992).

It is now generally accepted that graduated, sustained compression therapy is the treatment of choice for patients suffering from venous ulceration (NHS Centre for Reviews and Dissemination, 1997). The main methods include (Morison et al, 1998):

- ▶ single layer inelastic bandages
- ▶ single layer elastic bandages
- ▶ multilayer bandage systems
- ▶ compression stockings/hosiery

Inelastic bandages

These are generally made of cotton and applied at 90% extension. They apply a semi-rigid support to the calf muscle. Sub-bandage pressures will vary depending on the patient's level of activity: during periods of exercise the pressure may rise steeply, while at rest the pressure has been recorded as comparatively low (Morison et al, 1998).

Elastic bandages

These bandages contain an elastomer that helps to sustain applied compression over a longer period. They are generally applied at 50% extension, but if this is varied the sub-bandage pressure will increase or decrease. They are capable of exerting either medium or high levels of compression and, as with all bandages, the manufacturer's instructions must be read carefully before application, especially if applying the bandage for the first time.

Multilayer systems

These bandage systems are made of a variety of types of bandage. As well as non-compression layers such as orthopaedic wool and crêpe bandage, they incorporate a number of compression bandages that have the cumulative effect of providing the desired pressure. It could be argued that this combination of bandages is less likely to result in potentially excessive sub-bandage pressure.

Compression stockings/hosiery

These are mainly used to control oedema, manage varicose veins, and for the prevention and treatment of venous disorders. They are generally accepted to be much safer than inappropriately applied high-compression bandages, as the pressure profiles of the stockings are known (as a result of testing). A range of compression profiles is available to suit the needs of different patients. They are more cosmetically acceptable and useful in preventing recurrence of venous ulceration, provided that they are correctly fitted and the patient is able to apply them (Moffatt and O'Hare, 1995b).

Compression therapy – general information

Compression therapy, however achieved, aims to provide graduated compression, with the highest pressure at the ankle and the lowest at the knee. Stemmer (1969) recommended that in order to reverse the effects of chronic venous hypertension a pressure of between 35mmHg and 40mmHg was required at the ankle reducing to approximately 17mmHg just below the knee.

Moffatt and Harper (1997) have reported that these pressures have not yet proved to be optimal; however, if ankle pressure exceeds 60mmHg then patient compliance can be a problem and the risk of pressure necrosis increases.

The natural shape of most legs facilitates graduated compression. The circumference of the lower limb generally increases towards the knee. The beneficial effects of graduated compression are summarised in Box 2. It could be argued that the longer the compression remains in place, the greater the benefits to the patient.

> ► Reduces superficial vein distension
>
> ► Improves competency of damaged valve function (in some patients)
>
> ► Enhances blood flow through the deep veins
>
> ► Mimics the action of the calf muscle pump by providing an external force on the expanding muscle, thereby deflecting the internal pressure caused by muscle expansion back onto the venous system
>
> ► Reduces the presence or build-up of oedema by forcing fluid back into both the venous and lymphatic systems

Box 2 The beneficial effects of graduated compression

The RCN's clinical practice guidelines on managing patients with venous leg ulcers acknowledge the strength of evidence in favour of compression therapy. The findings of an expert panel, with members drawn from the RCN Institute, Centre for Evidence-Based Nursing at York University and Manchester University School of Nursing, recommend: 'Graduated multilayer high compression systems, with adequate padding, capable of sustaining compression for at least a week should be the first line of treatment for uncomplicated venous leg ulcers' (RCN et al, 1998).

In addition, the guidelines acknowledge that more research is required to identify the training strategies that will improve compression bandaging techniques for the longest possible period of time and that therefore, in the meantime, compression bandage systems should only be applied by trained practitioners.

Summary

Before using compression therapy a practitioner should understand how the bandage works and how to apply it. This is particularly important because the effects of inappropriately applied compression therapy are potentially harmful (Callam et al, 1987b).

Quality of life as an outcome indicator

Research studies undertaken within the last decade have suggested that, in addition to the usual indicators of successful care interventions and outcomes (for example, the time taken to achieve healing), an analysis of the impact of the ulcer on the patient's quality of life is an appropriate outcome indicator (Franks et al, 1994).

There are a number of tools available with which to measure quality of life. One of the most relevant has been developed by Hyland et al (1994). The four main areas of the patient's lifestyle considered particularly relevant are: pain; restricted activity; moods and feelings; the patient's preoccupation with their ulcer and associated treatment regimes.

Recently, research identified that leg ulceration has a bigger impact on perceived quality of life in younger patients and confirmed that the impact is greater for men than women (Franks and Moffatt, 1998).

Franks (1998) suggests that, as the NHS continues to move towards evidence-based practice and audit, there is a clear need to assess the impact of disease on patients' quality of life. But further studies into the use of quality of life measures are needed before they can be considered an integral part of the assessment process for all patients with chronic wounds.

Conclusion

Although there have been many advances in knowledge and practice regarding patients with venous leg ulcers, many questions still have to be answered, especially related to pathology and development. This chapter has introduced some of the relevant issues as well as indicating the level of knowledge and understanding required for practitioners truly to act as the patient's advocate and ensure best practice in the light of current research.

References

Bale, S. (1997) A guide to wound debridement. *Journal of Wound Care*; 6: 4, 179–182.

Bosanquet, N. (1992) Cost of venous ulcers: from maintenance therapy to investment programmes. *Phlebology*; Supplement 1: 44–46.

Bosanquet, N. et al (1993) Community leg ulcer clinics: cost effectiveness. *Health Trends*; 25: 4, 145.

Callam, M. et al (1985) Chronic ulceration of the leg: extent of the problem and provision of care. *British Medical Journal*; 290: 1855–1856.

Callam, M. (1987a) Arterial disease in chronic leg ulceration: an underestimated hazard? Lothian and Forth Valley Leg Ulcer Study. *British Medical Journal*; 294: 6577, 929–931.

Callam, M. et al (1987b) Hazards of compression treatment of the leg: an estimate from Scottish surgeons. *British Medical Journal*; 295: 6610, 1382.

Cameron, J. (1992) *Leg Ulcers: Aetiology and Differential Diagnosis* (Educational Leaflet 8). Huntingdon: Wound Care Society.

Collier, M. (1994) Assessing a wound (RCN Nursing Update, Unit 29). *Nursing Standard*; 7: 20, supplement, 3–8.

Collier, M. (1996a) Leg ulceration: a review of causes and treatment. *Nursing Standard*; 10: 31, 49–51.

Collier, M. (1996b) Principles of optimum wound management. *Nursing Standard*; 10: 43, 47–52.

Cornwall, J. et al (1986) Leg ulcers: epidemiology and aetiology. *British Journal of Surgery*; 73: 693–696.

Dale, J. et al (1983) Chronic ulcers of the leg: a study of prevalence in a Scottish community. *Health Bulletin*; 41: 310–314.

Dale, J. (1995) The anatomy and physiology of the circulation of the leg. In: Cullum, N., Roe, B. (eds) *Leg Ulcers: Nursing Management: – A Research Based Guide.* London: Scutari.

Flanagan, M. (1997) *Wound Management* (ACE Series). Edinburgh: Churchill Livingstone.

Franks, P. (1998) Quality of life as an outcome indicator. In: Morison, M. et al (eds) *Nursing Management of Chronic Wounds.* London: C.V. Mosby.

Franks, P. et al (1994) Community leg ulcer clinics: effect on quality of life. *Phlebology*; 9: 83–86.

Franks, P., Moffatt, C. (1998) Who suffers most from leg ulceration? *Journal of Wound Care*; 7: 8, 383–385.

Gaylarde, P. et al (1993) The effect of compression on venous stasis. *British Journal of Dermatology*; 128: 3, 255–258.

Hinchliff, S., Montague, S. (1988) *Physiology for Nursing Practice.* London: Baillière Tindall.

Hyland, M. et al (1994) Quality of life of leg ulcer patients: questionnaire and preliminary findings. *Journal of Wound Care*; 3: 6, 294–298.

Laing, W. (1992*) Chronic Venous Diseases of the Leg.* London: Office of Health Economics.

Miller, M., Dyson, M. (1996) *Principles of Wound Care.* London: Macmillan.

Moffatt, C. (1992) Compression bandaging – the state of the art. *Journal of Wound Care*; 1: 1, 45–50.

Moffatt, C., O'Hare, L. (1995a) Ankle pulses are not sufficient to detect impaired arterial circulation in patients with leg ulcers. *Journal of Wound Care*; 4: 3, 134–138.

Moffatt, C., O'Hare, L. (1995b) Graduated compression hosiery for venous ulceration. *Journal of Wound Care*; 4: 10, 459.

Moffatt, C., Harper, P. (1997) *Leg Ulcers* (ACE series). Edinburgh: Churchill Livingstone.

Morison, M. et al (1998) *Nursing Management of Chronic Wounds.* London: C.V. Mosby.

RCN et al (1998) *Clinical Practice Guidelines: The Management of Patients with Venous Leg Ulcers.* London: RCN Publishing.

NHS Centre for Reviews and Dissemination (1997) *Effective Health Care Bulletin*; Vol. 3, No. 2. York: NHS Centre for Reviews and Dissemination.

Stemmer, R. (1969) Ambulatory-elasto-compressive treatment of the lower extremities particularly with elastic stockings. *Kassenarzt*; 9: 1–8.

Tortora, G., Anagnostakos, N. (1987) *Principles of Anatomy and Physiology* (5th edition). New York: Harper International.

Vowden, K. et al (1996) Hand-held Doppler assessment for peripheral arterial assessment. *Journal of Wound Care*; 5: 3, 125-128.

7 Diabetic ulceration

Ali Foster

Key points

▶ The key to successful treatment of the patient with diabetic foot disease is multidisciplinary care

▶ There are two distinct types of diabetic foot syndrome – the neuropathic foot and the neuro-ischaemic foot

▶ Diagnosis of underlying disease aetiology is essential for effective treatment

▶ Treatment of neuropathic ulceration should include offloading of pressure, sharp debridement, control of infection and regular reassessment

▶ Treatment of iscaemic ulceration will involve appropriate vascular intervention, special footwear, judicious sharp debridement and infection control

Introduction

Diabetic foot disease is a major public health problem. Although people with diabetes make up just 2% of the population, this minority group will undergo 50% of major amputations of a leg (Edmonds, 1996).

In order to reduce this unacceptably high morbidity, a specialist approach to healing and prevention needs to be established. Work over the past two decades indicates that the key to successful treatment is multidisciplinary care by a team that includes a nurse. A team that can offer early detection of complications by screening, careful diagnosis, care of lesions, preventive education and follow-up within the forum of a diabetic foot clinic can reduce major amputations by at least 50% (Edmonds et al, 1986).

But even when such a forum is available, organising access to care is not always straightforward. Diabetic foot patients are often elderly, frail and socially isolated. Most significantly, they lack the protective pain sensation that should warn them that something is wrong. Furthermore, there are few specialist multidisciplinary diabetic foot clinics.

As in many areas of medicine, the evidence base for establishing what is 'state of the art' management of diabetic foot lesions is small. For this reason, many nurses working with diabetic foot ulceration are tempted to extrapolate from wound care experience in other fields. However, when dealing with the insensitive diabetic foot this could lead to management problems. The diabetic foot lesion is a unique entity requiring special management. Therefore, health care professionals should not work in isolation when they are dealing with diabetic foot patients.

In the case of the diabetic foot, the presence of neuropathy, ischaemia and immunosuppression in various combinations has profound implications for management. These factors are present in diabetic foot patients, and it is for these reasons that morbidity is so unacceptably high.

Diabetic foot syndromes

There are two distinct types of diabetic foot syndrome, and treatment will depend on which is present. First, the neuropathic foot, where damage to the nerves leads to lack of protective pain sensation, but the blood supply to the foot is good. Rapid healing can be achieved with suitable treatment. Second, the neuro-ischaemic foot, where there is a combination of neuropathy and poor blood supply. In these cases, healing can be very protracted.

Occasionally one encounters a purely ischaemic diabetic foot with no significant degree of neuropathy. These patients should be treated in the same way as those with neuro-ischaemia, and again, healing can be slow (Edmonds et al, 1986).

The neuropathic foot

Patients with neuropathy have nerve damage in their feet and lower limbs. The cause is chronic hyperglycaemia and the affected nerves no longer transmit the sensations of heat, cold or pain (Boulton, 1998). Patients with neuropathy feel no discomfort when they injure their feet or develop a foot infection. Because of this lack of pain they will walk freely upon an open wound which will prevent ulcers from closing. They will be unaware if their shoes are too tight or if they step on a sharp object that penetrates their shoe.

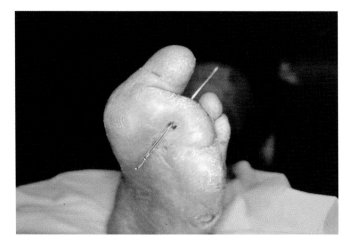

A probe inserted through this tracking ulcer is not painful for the patient because of neuropathy. Two toes are missing, suggesting previous arterial disease

The consequences of neuropathy are threefold. First, the patient may simply not perceive that there is an ulcer on the foot, since the pain that would normally alert him to the problem is absent. Second, even if the patient knows that there is an ulcer, the absence of pain may lead him to neglect the problem and fail to seek treatment. In a foot which has protective pain sensation, injury will lead to loss of function. The neuropathic patient will continue to walk.

Third, the patient will not complain. Nurses and other members of the health care team are trained to respond to a patient's complaints. It is pain and complaining which lead us to perceive the problem. If pain is absent, there is a risk that the seriousness of the situation will be underestimated.

Patients with diabetes who attend for a routine appointment or an annual review should never simply be asked whether they have any foot problems. All diabetic patients should have a foot inspection at every clinic visit. They should regularly be screened for the presence of neuropathy and ischaemia and foot lesions (Caputo et al, 1994, Klenerman et al, 1996).

Diagnosis of the neuropathic foot

This can be done cheaply and quickly by means of a simple 5.07 monofilament which is held perpendicular to the foot and pressed until it buckles at a given force of 10g (Kumar et al, 1991). Many pharmaceutical companies will now supply these filaments free of charge.

If the patient can feel the pressure of a 10g monofilament, then protective pain sensation is present. Several different sites on both feet should be tested, and it is best to perform the test after callus has been removed from the test site, otherwise a false negative result may be recorded. Patients who fail the test will need careful education in trauma prevention, regular foot checks and early reporting of problems.

There are other signs of neuropathy which should alert the practitioner (Foster and Edmonds, 1987). Neuropathic feet are warm and well perfused. The skin is often dry, because autonomic neuropathy leads to diminished sweating. Pulses can be palpated easily and patients often complain that their feet feel tight or tingling and may mention a subjective feeling of coldness. The veins on the top of the foot may be distended because of arterio-venous shunting.

It is essential for nurses to be aware that their patients have neuropathy. If protective pain sensation is absent, special strategies must be devised to protect the patient from unperceived trauma.

The neuro-ischaemic foot

Neuro-ischaemic patients have a combination of neuropathy and ischaemia. Their vascular disease tends to be bilateral, multi-segmental and distal. The consequences of ischaemia are twofold. Without adequate blood flow, patients cannot mount the vascular component of the inflammatory response, so their wounds do not heal. Second, they cannot fight infection effectively. When, together with their ischaemia they also have neuropathy, the results can be catastrophic. Such neuro-ischaemic patients often have no symptoms such as intermittent claudication or rest pain to warn them that something is wrong. They can progress to ulceration or gangrene with no warning symptoms.

Diagnosis of the neuro-ischaemic foot

A useful clinical tool to confirm the presence of ischaemia is a small hand-held Doppler which can be used with a sphygmomanometer to measure the brachial systolic pressure and the ankle systolic pressure. If the ankle systolic pressure is lower than that in the arm, then the patient is ischaemic (Foster and Edmonds, 1987). Patients with absent foot pulses who develop pain or ulceration should be referred without delay to a hospital foot clinic for urgent vascular review.

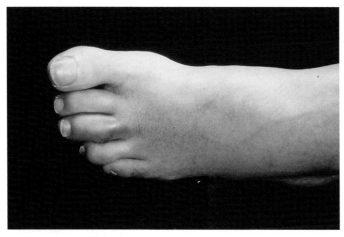

Cellulitic third toe and foot in a neuropathic patient

Problems with diagnosing ischaemia

Practitioners should always remember that the presence of concurrent neuropathy will prevent some patients from developing symptoms of ischaemia. Many will never suffer from cramping of the calves on walking (intermittent claudication) or rest pain, even though they are severely ischaemic. Again, the absence of pain can cloud the issue and lead both patient and carer to underestimate the problem. All diabetic patients should, therefore, be screened for ischaemia (Fowler and Mitchell, 1998).

Some patients with ischaemia will suffer from medial calcification of their arteries which stiffens the arterial wall (Gibbons et al, 1995). It cannot be compressed by the sphygomanometer cuff and, therefore, the systolic pressure reading will be artificially high. Clinicians should be aware of this potential problem when they are assessing patients for ischaemia. Such patients, whose feet appear ischaemic but who have high pressures on Doppler, should be referred to a vascular laboratory for further studies.

Neuro-ischaemic feet are usually cold, although some will appear to be a healthy, bright pink colour as their capillaries, in an attempt to oxygenate the foot, are distended. They may be painful depending on the degree of concurrent neuropathy. They are pale when elevated but when dependent may develop rubor or cyanosis.

If a major artery is suddenly occluded the foot will become greyish with purple mottling. The patient may complain of severe pain or numbness and weakness in the affected limb. This presentation is rare, but it is a clinical emergency. Without vascular intervention the limb may be lost. The patient should be referred to a hospital with a vascular surgical facility without delay. It is essential for practitioners to be aware of peripheral vascular disease. Without this knowledge, optimal wound care is not possible.

Neuropathic ulcers

Trauma can cause ulceration on any part of the foot of a neuropathic patient. However, the classic neuropathic ulcer develops on the sole of the foot where the pressure is high when the patient walks. Usually the foot responds to such increased pressure by developing a callus. If the callus becomes very thick, the underlying tissue will be injured and an ulcer is likely to develop.

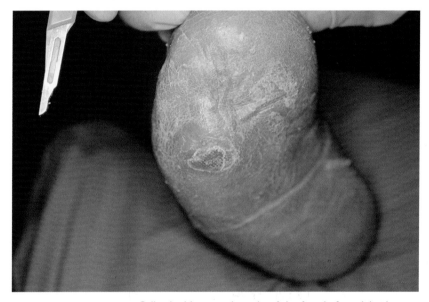

Callus build-up on the sole of the foot before debridement

The first sign that this is happening will be the development of speckles of blood within the callus, where capillaries subjected to pressure begin to leak their contents. If this is not excised, further damage will occur as the callus grows and a bulla of sero-sanguinous fluid will develop. This is actually a collection of exudate from a hidden ulcer. Without treatment a sinus will eventually form and fluid will be discharged from the ulcer (Foster, 1991).

Neuropathic ulcers are prone to infection which can enter the foot and spread with alarming rapidity, leading to further tissue destruction. In many cases the patient is unaware of what is happening. Daily inspection of the feet for callus, colour changes and fluid leakage is therefore essential for the prevention and early detection of neuropathic ulcers. If the pre-ulcerative state is detected early enough, removal of callus and relief of excessive plantar pressure can prevent ulceration.

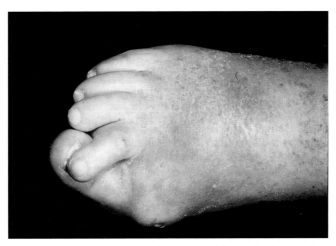

Cellulitis in deformed ischaemic foot

Chronic overloading of plantar sites will cause neuropathic ulcers and prevent healing (Veves, 1992). Once the skin of the neuropathic foot is broken by trauma, then pressure offloading is essential to achieve healing (Frykberg, 1997).

In the foot with normal sensation, even a small and superficial lesion will cause acute pain on walking. Pain sensation thus protects wounds from further trauma. Walking causes pressure, friction, and shear and sets up a non-healing cycle which must be broken to achieve tissue repair. We must either prevent neuropathic patients from weight-bearing or provide methods of reducing the plantar pressures.

In appearance, neuropathic ulcers are very distinctive lesions. They are surrounded and overlaid by yellowish callus. If the callus is soaked in exudate from the ulcer it will be white and moist. The dimensions of neuropathic ulcers may be deceptive. A sterile probe or a swab can be passed to detect hidden depths and undermined areas. If the probe reaches bone, this is a sign of underlying osteomyelitis (Grayson et al, 1995). Neuropathic ulcers are usually painless.

Treatment of neuropathic ulceration involves immediate offloading of pressure, sharp debridement, control of infection and provision of regular dressings and inspection (Foster, 1991). The metabolic state of the patient should also be examined and if diabetic control is poor this should be addressed. It is important to remember that in addition to achieving rapid healing of the ulcer we have to try to prevent relapse in the future.

Pressure relief of neuropathic ulcers

There are many techniques for achieving offloading of ulcerated feet. Some are, in theory, very simple, such as confining the patient to strict bed rest or using crutches or a wheelchair. However, patients do not take kindly to this limitation of normal activity, particularly when they have a problem which causes no pain and are young and active.

Other techniques used will allow for walking and are chosen with the understanding that it is impossible for some patients to take to their beds for the duration of the ulcer. Such techniques include the provision of special shoes and insoles (Tovey, 1985; Uccioli et al, 1995), Scotchcast boots (Burden et al, 1983), total contact casts (Coleman et al, 1984) and Aircasts™ (Foster et al,

8 Pressure ulcer development and principles for prevention

Mark Collier

Key points

▶ Variables associated with the development of pressure ulcers can be defined as intrinsic, extrinsic, primary or secondary

▶ Pressure, shear and friction forces are responsible for pressure damage

▶ Prevention of pressure damage is the primary objective

▶ Risk assessment tools should be used as part of a prevention strategy

▶ Health care professionals need to have a working knowledge of support services to effect pressure relief and reduction

Introduction

The aim of this chapter is to introduce readers to the theory of pressure ulcer (PU) development. It will outline some of the associated research and clarify some fundamental concepts underpinning rationales for current pressure ulcer guidelines and care pathways.

First, what is a pressure ulcer? It can be defined as 'an ulceration of the skin due to the effects of prolonged pressure in combination with a number of other variables' (Collier, 1995; Collier, 1996; EUPAP, 1997). The other variables may be intrinsic or extrinsic in nature (Box 1). There may also be primary or secondary factors which increase an individual's risk of developing a pressure ulcer (Box 1).

Intrinsic An identifiable factor within the patient that increases the risk of PU development, such as ischaemia or nutritional status

Extrinsic An identifiable factor external to the patient that increases the risk of PU development, such as position or nature and state of the support surface

Primary A factor (specific to an individual) which increases their risk of PU development, such as immobility or skin condition

Secondary A factor (specific to the individual) such as skin infection or maceration associated with the risk of PU development as opposed to directly responsible for it

Note: Primary or secondary factors vary depending on the client group being assessed. What is a primary factor for an elderly patient, for example, immobility, may be a secondary factor for a paediatric patient

Previously the terms 'decubitus ulcer', 'pressure sore' and 'bedsore' have been used to describe pressure ulcers, especially in American literature (Krasner, 1990). However, as previously explained, these terms are thought to have originated from the observation that ulcers and sores frequently occurred in people who were bedridden (Collier, 1995)

Decubitus is a derivative of the Latin word *decumbo*, which means to lie down. It is becoming more common to use the term pressure ulcer, as this more correctly reflects the pathogenesis (Bader, 1990).

Box 1 Variables associated with the development of pressure ulcers

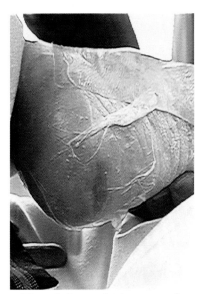

Plate 1 A superficial pressure ulcer

Defining 'pressure'

Bennett and Lee (1986) defined pressure as 'a perpendicular load or force (for example, patient's body weight) being exerted on a unit of area (for example, the buttocks)'. This is also referred to as compression. They went on to demonstrate that pressure could be accurately measured using the formula pressure equals force over surface area or by the use of pressure-sensitive equipment such as a pressure monitor. The results are known as interface pressures.

Shear, friction and moisture are other mechanisms involved in the formation of PUs.

Shear – *a mechanical stress that is parallel to a plane of interest* (Bennett and Lee, 1986)

Bennett and Lee found that only half the amount of pressure is needed to produce damage if a relatively high level of shear is present. When describing the effect of shear, many authors have noted that there is a greater compressive force placed on sacral tissues when the head of a bed is elevated (Berecek, 1975; Brown et al, 1985; Reichel, 1958). It is thought that a 'shear' ulcer develops as a result of the patient's sacral skin adhering to bed linen. In the sitting position, owing to gravitational forces, the deep fascia moves downwards, while the sacral fascia remains attached to the sacral dermis.

This results in a stretching of the dermal microcirculation which, if unchecked, can lead to avulsion of local capillaries and arterioles, increasing the possibility of local tissue necrosis. Shear forces are exacerbated by surface moisture (Reichel, 1958).

Although shear can be defined separately from pressure, it is difficult to create pressure without shear and shear without pressure (Bridel, 1993).

Friction – *the force related to two surfaces moving across one another* (Krouskop, 1976)

Friction is not thought to be a primary factor in the development of PUs (Collier, 1997a), but it can exacerbate the stripping of broken epidermis or cause an initial break in the skin. This can be further compromised by the added effects of compression and shear forces. Safe and recommended moving and handling techniques will help to ensure the patient's skin remains intact.

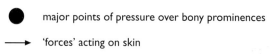

●   major points of pressure over bony prominences

⟶   'forces' acting on skin

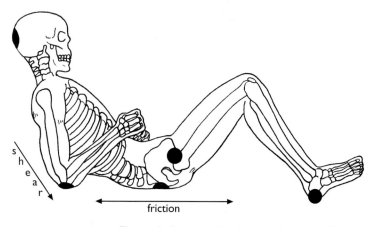

friction

Figure 1 Shear and friction can also cause damage

Moisture – *if the surface on which the patient is being supported is moist, studies have shown that the friction co-efficient will rise. If great enough this will lead to the patient's skin adhering to the damp surface, exacerbating damage* (Lothian et al, 1976)

In summary, the physical parameters that must be considered with reference to the aetiology of pressure ulcers are:

▶ pressure

▶ shear

▶ friction

▶ moisture

The development of PUs involves intrinsic, extrinsic, primary and secondary factors as well as these physical parameters (Collier, 1989; Bridel, 1993).

Measuring pressure

Although interface pressures are an important part of the theory of PU development, it is simplistic to regard these as absolute because results will vary depending upon the patient's weight, posture and the size and nature of the recording equipment, in particular the size of the transducers (Bader, 1990).

Following experimental studies involving a microinjection technique, Landis (1930) suggested that a value of 32mmHg was the mean capillary closing pressure of the arterial flow. Other studies suggested this figure should be higher (Barton and Barton, 1981; Daniel et al, 1981). In 1941 Landis revised his work using an amended technique. He identified the threshold over which damage was likely to occur as between 46mmHg and 50mmHg.

The relevance of this becomes clear when considering the interface pressures recorded between major bony prominences of a patient and the standard contract NHS mattress. These have been reported as between 70 and 100mmHg, thus exceeding capillary closing pressure (Collier, 1996).

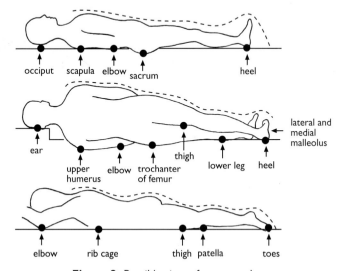

Figure 2 Possible sites of pressure damage

Other factors, aside from the patient's size and position, should be considered when measuring interface pressures. These include the surfaces creating the interface, which may be the skin and a mattress/cushion; the skin and a prosthesis; or the skin and an orthosis, for example, a surgical corset.

In addition, Lothian, as part of an unpublished thesis study (1983), highlighted the relationship between the amount of localised pressure and the longevity of its application.

Transmission of pressure

The external pressures at an interface are transmitted from the body surface to the underlying skeletal anatomy, compressing all the intermediate tissue. The resulting pressure gradient has been widely reported as the McClemont 'cone of pressure' (McClemont, 1984). This is defined as an increase of the external force at the point of greatest pressure on the bony surface. If the external pressure is recorded as 50mmHg, the pressure at the bony prominence rises to 200mmHg.

Because pressure is being distributed and amplified to deeper tissue, external skin ulcers, identified by classification tools such as Torrance (1983) or Collier (1989), may indicate that necrosis of underlying tissues is already becoming established. This explains why a sinus or cavity can be revealed under a superficial defect.

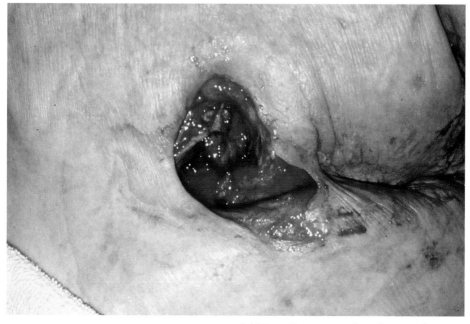

A high-grade pressure ulcer that is undermining

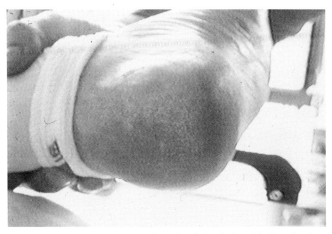

A patient's heel; the skin is unbroken

epidermis

dermis

A high-frequency ultrasound scan of the same patient's normal skin (cross-section)

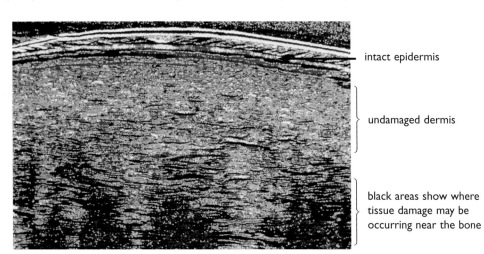

intact epidermis

undamaged dermis

black areas show where
tissue damage may be
occurring near the bone

A high-frequency ultrasound scan over the patient's heel
demonstrating areas of possible tissue damage near the bone

The normal physiological response to pressure

In the dermis, capillary loops run vertical to the surface and are coiled at their bases, limiting the risk of occlusion from direct pressure. In the subcutaneous tissues, however, blood vessels lie mainly in parallel planes, making them more vulnerable to distortion and occlusion. It has been reported that as little as five seconds' occlusion of blood flow can provoke an evident reaction which may last anywhere between a third and three-quarters the period of ischaemia (Bliss, 1993). This is known as reactive hyperaemia.

With reference to the classic research undertaken by Lewis and Grant (1925), it is clear that the hyperaemic response is influenced by two processes:

▶ vasodilatory response to the complete cessation of arterial blood flow

▶ a superficial response to a transient diminution of blood flow in the affected anatomical region

It is also dependent upon the temperature of the relevant anatomical part (Lewis and Grant, 1925).

In some patients, vascular changes occur that can lead to the release of endotoxins in as little as 10 minutes. This may increase the risk of small vessels thrombosing under pressure (Freeman, 1906).

Prevention is better than cure

The philosophical basis for developing pressure ulcer prevention policies has been 'prevention is better than cure' (Munro, 1940). Various authors have endeavoured to identify the scale of the pressure ulcer problem in the NHS using data collected from prevalence or incidence studies (Department of Health, 1993). (A prevalence study is 'a snapshot in time which identifies the proportion of a defined population who have a pressure ulcer on the day or period of time in question'; an incidence study is 'a proportion of an identical population who develop a pressure ulcer over a period of time while receiving health care'.)

The NHS Executive estimated the incidence of pressure ulcers within hospital and community settings as 10% and 7% respectively and argued that many of these ulcers could be considered preventable (Livesley, 1994).

Cost implications

The total cost of PU treatment in the NHS has been estimated to be between £60m and £321m a year (Department of Health, 1991, 1993). In estimating treatment costs incurred for a typical patient with a grade 4/stage 5 pressure ulcer, Hibbs put both the direct and indirect costs at almost £26,000, in addition to the cost of the treatment for which the patient had originally been admitted (cited in Collier, 1989; Hibbs, 1990).

Using a similar formula to Hibbs, this figure has been updated from patient episodes at a major teaching hospital in Cambridgeshire (Collier, 1994) (Table 1). Treatment costs for PU of grades 0/1, 2 and 3 were identified as £2,500, £7,500 and £15,000–20,000 respectively.

Wound management materials (dressings)	£18.14	(per day)
Labour (time)	£10.00	(per day)
Specialty bed (hire)	£56.00	(average per day)
Pharmacy (one course of oral antibiotics)	£1.93	(per day)
Hotel (overheads only)	£50.00	(per day)
Staff (based on one E-grade, one doctor and one health care assistant being available)	£298.00	(per day)
Sub-total	£434.07	
Days to healing × 90		
Total	£39,066.30	
Source: Collier, 1994		

Table I Cost of treating a patient with a developed grade 4 pressure ulcer to healing

Prevention programme

The essentials of a prevention programme should include:

▶ education of the multidisciplinary team

▶ assessment and prediction of patients at risk

▶ assessment of existing ulcers and appropriate treatment

▶ delivery of quality care, identifying responsibility for setting standards of care and expected outcomes and ensuring the care is acceptable to the patient

Risk assessment

An analysis of the tools used to identify patients most at risk of developing PUs has been published elsewhere (Flanagan, 1993). No assessment tool can replace clinical observation and judgement (Bergstrom et al, 1986) but should be used alongside clinical skills. Likewise it could be argued that no tool can be truly effective unless it is used systematically, understood and interpreted in a similar manner by all those who use it and is not only used at admission.

Preventive patient management – a few ideas

In 1946 Guttman initiated the 'lifting and turning team' concept. He concluded that two hours appeared to be the maximum tolerance time of a patient's skin when maintained in the same position (Guttman, 1953).

With technological advances and improved availability of patient support surfaces, it is now generally accepted that two-hourly turning regimes need to be varied depending on the patient's medical and physical condition and the base support surface being used.

The turning clock is a simple formalisation of Guttman's idea that can be developed with the patient and incorporated into relevant nursing documentation.

The 30-degree tilt helps modify the patient's position using strategically placed pillows. It reduces pressure at the sacrum and may alleviate discomfort associated with more pronounced positional changes (Guttman, 1976).

The principles for the use of the 30-degree tilt are:

▶ maximum support

▶ protection of vulnerable areas

▶ sacral clearance from the support surface

▶ assistance with inspection of at-risk areas

▶ frequency of tilt is dictated by patient's clinical condition

▶ can be used alongside other simple aids to achieve maximum pressure reduction

Prevention need not necessarily involve major cost, and additional resources, in the shape of specific equipment, will not always be needed.

Place the patient in the centre of the bed with sufficient pillows to support the head and neck

Place a pillow at an angle under one buttock thus tilting the pelvis by 30°. Check with a flattened hand that the sacrum is just clear of the mattress

Place a pillow lengthways under each leg so that the heels are lifted clear of the bed

The 30° tilt

Pressure reduction or pressure relief?

Pressure reduction is the constant reduction in the amount of external pressure being exerted on a patient's anatomy while at rest, whereas pressure relief is intermittent lowering of the external pressure being exerted on the patient's anatomy (AHCPR, 1994).

Pressure reduction can be achieved either by moving the patient or by the use of a 'supportive' surface, for example, a static mattress with a two-way stretch cover that will conform more closely with the patient's body shape. In order for pressure reduction to be achieved over a prolonged period (30 minutes or more), both the previous concepts must be used together (AHCPR, 1994). Pressure relief, on the other hand, can be achieved using a 'dynamic' patient support system.

Equipment

Nowadays there is a vast array of support surfaces available. To decide which product is best suited to which patient, health care professionals need to have a working knowledge of products, their purpose and how they work.

Static overlays

The simplest form of pressure-reducing equipment available is an overlay mattress. This may be made of a foam, fibre or gel core. It conforms to the patient's body shape and helps redistribute weight over a larger surface area.

Static mattresses

A number of static mattresses with pressure-reducing properties are now available. Factors influencing choice may include:

▶ inner core foam density

▶ core construction of foam (single or composite, split or solid inner core)

▶ frequency of mattress turning required

▶ type of cover material

▶ best bed base for optimal performance

▶ cost and longevity

Static cushions

There are various pressure-reducing cushions available, but it is important to ensure the supportive qualities of the chosen cushion mirror those of any pressure-reducing mattress (Collier, 1997b).

Alternating pressure mattresses

These can be supplied as either overlays or replacement mattresses. In both cases they consist of a number of sealed cells, in a removable cover, that inflate and deflate alternately. Products differ in cell configuration, size, shape and identified cycle time.

Low air loss systems

These are available as both mattress and bed systems and provide pressure reduction via individual air-filled cells that are grouped regionally.

High air loss therapy

This is known generically as air fluidised therapy. In air fluidised mattresses warm air is circulated through a deep bed of ceramic beads. They tend to be used mainly in clinical areas such as burns or intensive therapy units.

Natural sheepskins

These can reduce friction and shear forces but do not reduce compression forces. Synthetic sheepskins have been shown to be non-effective and poor laundering can increase interface pressure (Lothian and Barbenal, 1983).

Other devices

These include bed cradles, monkey poles, patient hoists, foam wedges and troughs. Sorbo foam rings and/or pillows should never be used to reduce pressure as they concentrate pressure towards a point and may cause new pressure ulcers (Lothian and Barbenel, 1983).

Conclusion

To ensure optimum preventive health care is provided for patients, in whichever healthcare setting, it is important that all practitioners have a fundamental understanding of the concepts of pressure, pressure reduction/relief, prevention strategies and factors relative to the development of pressure ulcers so that they can make informed choices about the nature and type of equipment required.

References

Agency for Health Care Policy and Research (1994) *Treatment of Pressure Ulcers: Clinical Practice Guideline No. 15.* USA: AHCPR.

Bader, D. (ed.) (1990) *Pressure Sores: Clinical Practice and Scientific Approach.* London: Macmillan.

Barton, A., Barton, M. (1981) *The Management of Pressure Sores.* London: Faber.

Bennett, L., Lee, B. (1986) Shear versus pressure as causative factors in skin blood flow occlusion. *Archives of Physical of Medicine Rehabilitation*; 60: 309–314.

Berecek, K. (1975) Aetiology of pressure sores. *Clinics of North America*; 10: 157.

Bergstrom, N. et al (1986) Adequacy of descriptive scales for reporting dietary intake in the institutionalised elderly. *Journal Nutrition for Elderly*; 6: 1, 3–16.

Bliss, M. (1993) Aetiology of pressure sores. *Clinical Gerontology*; 3: 379–397.

Bridel, J. (1993) The aetiology of pressure sores. *Journal of Wound Care*; 2: 4, 230–238.

Brown, M. et al (1985) Nursing innovation for prevention of decubitus ulcers in long-term facilities. *Plastic Surgery Nurse*; 5: 2, 57.

Collier, M. (1989) *Pressure Sore Development and Prevention.* Leaflet 3 (1). Northampton: Wound Care Society.

Collier, M. (1994) *Quality Assurance Report.* Cambridge: Addenbrooke's Hospital.

Collier, M. (1995) *Pressure Sore Development and Prevention.* Educational Leaflet 3 (1). Northampton: Wound Care Society.

Collier, M. (1996) Pressure-reducing mattresses. *Journal of Wound Care*; 5: 5, 207–211.

Collier, M. (1997a) Aetiology of pressure ulcers. *Journal of Wound Care Resource File.* London: Emap.

Collier, M. (1997b) Taking the pressure off twenty-four hours a day! *Huntleigh Healthcare Clinical Report.* Luton: Huntleigh Nurse Education.

Daniel, R. el al (1981) Etiologic factors in pressure sores: an experimental model. *Archives of Physical Medicine Rehabilitation*; 62: 492–498.

Department of Health (1991) *The Health of the Nation.* London: HMSO.

Department of Health (1993) *Pressure Sores: A Key Quality Indicator.* DoH Publications.

EUPAP (1997) *Proceedings of the First European Pressure Ulcer Advisory Panel.* Oxford: EUPAP Conference.

Flanagan, M. (1993) Pressure sore risk assessment scales. *Journal of Wound Care*; 2: 3, 162–167.

Freeman, L. (1906) Clinical forms of gangrene: bedsores or decubitus? In Keen, W. (ed.) *Surgery: Its Principles and Practice.* USA.

Guttman, L. (1953) The treatment and rehabilitation of patients with injuries of the spinal cord. In: Ope, Z. (ed.) *Medical History of the Second World War: Surgery,* Vol. 2. London: HMSO.

Guttman, L. (1976) The prevention and treatment of pressure sores. In Kenedi, R (ed.) *Bedsore Biomechanics.* London: Macmillan.

Hibbs, P. (1990) The economics of pressure sores. In: Bader, D. *Pressure Sores: Clinical Practice and Scientific Approach.* London: Macmillan.

Krasner, D. (ed.) (1990) *Chronic Wound Care.* Pennsylvania: Health Management Publications Inc.

Krouskop, T. (1976) Mechanisms of decubitus ulcer formation: a hypothesis. *Medical Hypothesis*; 4: 1, 37–39.

Landis, E. (I930) Micro-circulation studies of capillary blood pressure in human skin. *Heart*: 15, 209–228.

Lewis, T., Grant, R. (1925) Observations upon reactive hyperaemia in man. *Heart*; 12, 73–120.

Livesley, B. (1994) Foreword. *VFM Update.* NHS Executive No. 12: 2.

Lothian, P. et al (1976) Underpads in the prevention of decubitus. In: Kenedi, R. (ed.) *Bedsore Biomechanics.* London: Macmillan.

Lothian, P., Barbenal, J. (eds) (1983) Nursing aspects of pressure sore development. In *Pressure sores.* London: Macmillan.

McClemont, E. (1984) Pressure sores. *Nursing*; 2: 21, supplement.

Munro, D. (1940) Care of the back following spinal cord injuries: a consideration of bed sores. *New England Journal of Medicine*; 223: 1, 391–398.

Reichel, S. (1958) Shearing forces as a factor in decubitus ulcer formation: an hypothesis. *Medical Hypothesis*; 4: 1, 37–39.

Torrance, C. (1983) *Pressure Sores: Aetiology, Treatment and Prevention.* London: Croom Helm.

9 Wound infection

Brian Gilchrist

Key points

- ▶ Wound infection is a problem because it delays wound healing
- ▶ Defining the term infection is important
- ▶ The presence of bacteria does not necessarily constitute infection
- ▶ Wound swabs will not diagnose infection
- ▶ Identification of clinical signs of infection is essential for diagnosis
- ▶ Not all clinical signs are associated with a wound infection

Introduction

The skin is the largest organ in the human body and in its normal state is home to a wide variety of bacteria. These bacteria (the 'normal' flora) live in warm, moist sites and generally cause the host no problems on intact skin. When the skin is breached, for whatever reason, the resultant injury or wound may become inhabited by the skin's own bacteria or other bacteria from the environment, which may lead to the development of clinical infection.

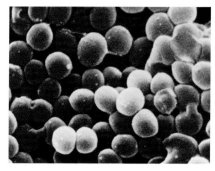

CINTI/CNR/Science Photo Library

Staphylococcus aureus

Wound infection is a problem because, at the most fundamental level, infection stops a wound from healing by:

▶ prolonging the inflammatory phase

▶ depleting the components of the complement cascade

▶ disrupting the normal clotting mechanisms

▶ promoting disordered leukocyte function and ultimately preventing the development of new blood vessels and formation of granulation tissue (Robson et al, 1990)

On a more serious level, infection may lead to further tissue breakdown and extension of the wound, such as in necrotising fasciitis (Neal, 1998), increased patient discomfort (especially in the form of more pain), disability, smell and other unpleasant symptoms and can lead to septicaemia and death. It is therefore of the utmost importance that the nurse involved in wound care understands how to identify wounds that are potentially infected and is able to institute appropriate measures to reduce the risk of further complications.

Identifying infection

One of the most problematic areas in any discussion about wound infection is the difficulty of deciding what constitutes an infected wound. The mere presence of bacteria does not indicate that a wound is infected. It is further complicated by two other factors: first, the observation that all chronic wounds contain bacteria; and second, the lack of any consensus about how to sample the bacteria which are present.

It is widely accepted that the one piece of information that is not a necessary criteria in diagnosing infection is the findings of a microbiological swab processed by a laboratory. There are a number of reasons for this:

▶ all chronic wounds contain bacteria and, in general, cultures show more than one species present (Gilchrist and Reed, 1989), often in very large numbers (Hutchinson, 1992). The bacteria that are found often represent either secondary colonisation or merely contamination

▶ false positives are not uncommon. The bacteria causing the infection are not the ones which are actually grown in the laboratory, and reported back to the clinical area. This may be especially true when the infection is caused by anaerobic bacteria (common in diabetic foot ulcers) which are very difficult to sample with a routine cotton-tip swab and which will generally not be present on the surface of an open lesion, where the atmospheric oxygen is toxic to them

Specimens for anaerobic culture need careful collection and immediate processing if they are to be of any use (Swann, 1985) and, as most chronic wounds are found in the community, swab results need to be interpreted with considerable caution.

The use of quantitative bacteriology (counting the number of bacteria present in a wound) has been suggested as a reliable way of defining wound infection (Stotts, 1995), and a rapid slide method for detecting infection in surgical wounds has also been described (Heggers, 1998). The problem is that these methods all depend on the use of biopsy specimens and costly laboratory services, and it is difficult to see this being of practical use to practitioners in community settings.

It is also doubtful how applicable such a system is to the most common wounds nurses deal with (leg ulcers and pressure sores) for two reasons: first, it has been shown that bacterial counts can show considerable variation across the surface of an ulcer (Schneider et al, 1983) and there is no agreement in the literature as to where on the wound surface the biopsy should be taken from; and second, such cultures do not give any information about invasion, nor do they take into account the cause and extent of the wound in relationship to the patient and the organism concerned (Thompson and Smith, 1994). We know, for example, that some bacteria, such as Streptococcus Group A, are considerably more virulent than others and that very small numbers can lead to catastrophic infections (Neal, 1994), while in other cases very large numbers appear to have no deleterious clinical effect (Hutchinson, 1992).

There is no agreement as to the 'correct' way to take a wound swab, thus increasing the possibility that the result will be unreliable (Gilchrist, l996). The microbial flora of a chronic wound is remarkably stable (Hansson et al, 1995) and studies in leg ulcers have shown that pre-treatment swabs provide no useful information as to the possible outcome of treatment (Eriksson et al, 1994).

As swabs are unreliable, and biopsies for the most part impractical, the wound care practitioner must depend instead on the presence of a host reaction (all the signs and symptoms associated with infection) as the only objective way of assessing a wound for potential infection. This is not always possible, as some wounds that are apparently infected (they heal when the patient is given antibiotics) display no obvious clinical signs other than the simple fact that they are not healing. This may be more pronounced in elderly people, as the general slowing down of their immune system means that they do not always mount a 'typical' immune response (Gilchrist, 1993).

In surgical wounds, the 'host reaction' most generally described is the presence of pus (Cruse and Foord, 1980) or purulent discharge associated with painful spreading erythema (Spencer, 1993). More commonly, the presence of clinical cellulitis (heat, redness, swelling and pain), sometimes associated with a pyrexia above 38°C, is familiar to most clinicians. There is little debate about the correct management: drainage of the pus, either by further surgery or by removal of all the stitches, prescription of systemic antibiotics and sometimes bed rest and elevation of the affected limb.

In the absence of clinical cellulitis, a common situation in the case of chronic wounds such as leg ulcers or pressure sores, other clinical signs must be sought. These have been described by Cutting and Harding (1994):

► presence of pus

► increased wetness

► change in pain

► change in appearance of granulation tissue

► odour

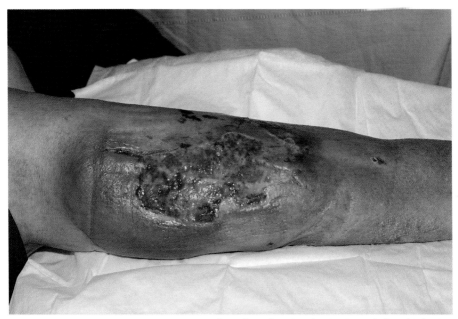

Leg ulcer showing classic signs of clinical infection

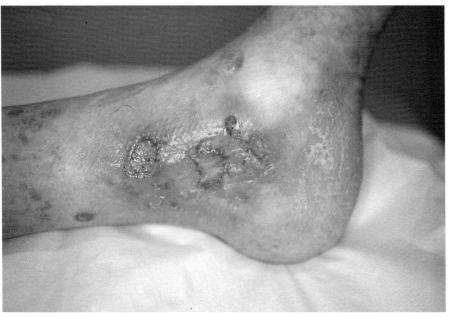

Leg ulcer with erythema only – this may not be infection as the
patient had no other clinical signs

Presence of pus

A clear sign of infection in an acute surgical wound, pus may also occur in a chronic wound, although it is not all that common, presumably because the open nature of the wound allows it to drain from the wound surface. Many hydrocolloid dressings dissolve to form an exudate not unlike pus in appearance, and it may be difficult to tell the two apart.

Increased wetness

Although there will be some exudate associated with most chronic wounds, normal granulation tissue is relatively dry. The sudden appearance of increased amounts of exudate in a healing wound may be an indicator of infection. This is due to the underlying capillaries dilating as part of the inflammatory response to allow white cells in particular to migrate to the source of the infection. In doing so the capillaries become leaky and allow greater quantities of plasma to leak out.

When a patient with a leg ulcer is seen for the first time, there is often considerable difficulty in determining whether or not the wetness generally seen in this situation is due to infection or the more likely causes of heart failure, with an associated cardiac oedema or oedema associated with uncontrolled venous hypertension. In the absence of any other symptoms, it is usual practice to rule out heart failure clinically and, assuming that the ulceration is due to venous disease, to apply suitable compression (and/or elevation) to treat the problem, rather than treating for clinical infection. Should the wetness persist, however, a course of antibiotics may be indicated.

Change in pain

In general a change in pain is an indicator that something untoward is occurring in a wound, but although this might be a sign that the wound has become infected, great care should be taken to rule out other causes first. Despite earlier suggestions that many chronic wounds are not painful, it is now clear that all chronic wounds are, in fact, associated with some degree of pain, albeit often manageable with simple analgesia (Cullum and Roe, 1995). The onset of a more acute pain should alert the clinician to be on the look-out for a cause.

As a first step, ischaemia should be ruled out by repeated measurement of the resting ankle pressure index (Vowden et al, 1996). If this is unchanged, the use of systemic antibiotics may be indicated. In the absence of other symptoms, there are other wound care situations where an investigation for ischaemia will also be merited: in the case of pressure sores the clinician must be assured that a suitable pressure-relieving device is being used; in the case of rheumatoid disease it must be established that the increase in pain is not an indicator of worsening disease, or the presence of vasculitis.

Naturally, ulceration with an underlying ischaemic cause (for example, peripheral vascular disease or diabetes) is itself especially prone to infection, especially anaerobic infection (Finegold, 1982). In this situation a prompt diagnosis must be made if serious consequences are to be avoided.

Change in the appearance of granulation tissue

As well as increased wetness, infected granulation tissue often becomes a darker colour and may be more friable, with a tendency to bleed more easily.

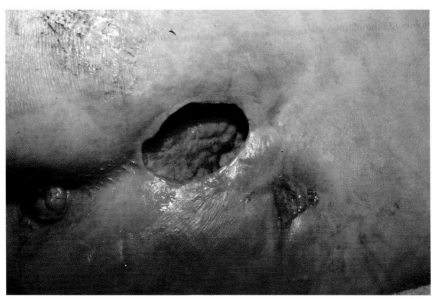

Dull red granulation tissue in a non-healing pressure ulcer

Odour

All wounds have some smell associated with them; however, the presence of any offensive odour should alert the clinician to the possibility of infection. Infections caused by anaerobic bacteria often produce an acrid or putrid smell owing to the presence of necrotic tissue. It may difficult to decide, for example, in the case of fungating carcinomas, whether the smell is due to infection, as defined above, or simply caused by colonisation, which is the most likely situation.

Treating patients with infected wounds

Before considering the local treatment of any wound, the nurse must first ensure that any risk factors associated with infection are either controlled or eradicated. It is necessary to ensure that a full and detailed history has been taken and that a clinical examination has been performed.

Too often 'treatment' appears to consist solely of sending off a swab and changing the dressing. When the patient's condition fails to improve, the dressing is blamed and another one takes its place. Failure to identify other factors will increase the likelihood of the wound not healing, as 'neither aseptic techniques nor the use of antibiotics has properly recognised that resistance to bacterial invasion depends almost entirely on the efficiency of the host's natural defence mechanisms' (Burke, 1980). It is essential to first answer the question: 'What caused this wound?' Wounds are a symptom, not a disease, and before any treatment is contemplated a definitive diagnosis should be attempted.

Although this may sometimes prove rather elusive, in many cases correct identification of the cause of the wound will lead to a rational treatment approach and subsequent healing.

Factors increasing the risk of infection

There are many factors which contribute to decreased resistance to infection, and any number of these can lead to a chronic, non-healing wound (Tobin, 1984; Leaper, 1995). They include:

▶ the presence of a foreign body in the wound (pieces of discarded dressing, especially gauze and tulle, dirt, suture material, drains)

▶ the presence of dead tissue, as a smaller number of bacteria are needed to cause infection

▶ contused tissue

▶ tissue ischaemia

▶ previous or current irradiation

▶ presence of a haematoma

▶ the use of vasoconstricting drugs

There are also a number of medical conditions which are known to predispose patients to infection and these include:

▶ diabetes

▶ cancer

▶ rheumatoid arthritis

▶ excessive alcohol intake

▶ malnourishment

▶ conditions which lead to suppressed or non-functioning of the immune system

▶ systemic use of steroids or antibiotics

▶ co-existing distant skin lesions such as exfoliative dermatitis, which themselves easily become the target of superficial infection (Lauria, 1985)

In addition, it should not be forgotten that the most significant preventable risk factor for surgical wound infection continues to be pre-operative shaving (Mishriki et al, 1990).

Removal of bacteria

There is little evidence that it is necessary to remove bacteria from the surface of a chronic wound for it to heal. It is now well accepted that sterility of the wound surface is neither a necessary condition for healing, nor is it actually possible. It has been shown that experimental wounds healed despite the presence of large numbers of bacteria in the fluid of occluded tissue (Mertz and Eaglestein, 1984). Clinical studies on leg ulcers have shown that the presence of bacteria did not hinder wound healing (Eriksson et al, 1994; Blair et al, 1988; Gilchrist and Reed, 1989), although one study (Trengove et al, 1996) did show that wound healing was impaired in leg ulcers if more than four different species were present.

Use of topical antibacterial agents

There appear to be a number of reasons given in the literature why the use of topical antibacterial agents is not generally advocated in chronic wound care (Selwyn, 1981). These suggest that antibacterial agents may lead to:

▶ local cell and tissue damage

▶ systemic toxicity

▶ the development of contact sensitivity and allergic reactions

▶ disturbances in the normal skin ecology, leading to super-infection and the possibility of developing antibiotic resistance

▶ interactions with other concurrent drug therapy, especially steroids

The use of topical antibiotics in chronic wound care has been advocated where it has been shown quantitatively that more than 10^5 bacteria per gram of tissue are present (Robson, 1991). However this form of treatment remains controversial as clinical studies have shown that topical silver sulphadiazine, for example, confers no benefit in wound healing over simple occlusion (Hutchinson, 1992), even in wounds where counts were shown to be higher than 10^5.

A recent review concluded: 'Topical antibiotics are inappropriate for wounds and ulcers although they are widely promoted for this purpose. We know of no controlled trials… showing their superiority' (*Drug and Therapeutics Bulletin*, 1991).

An exception to this may be in the specific case of grossly malodorous wounds such as fungating malignant lesions, where the use of topically applied metronidazole gel has been shown to be effective in reducing or preventing odour *(Lancet, 1990)*. At present the use of antibiotics is only advocated where clinical infection is present, and they should be administered systemically. It may be prudent to treat for anaerobes, even where none have been demonstrated, but the specific choice of antibiotic(s) will depend on local prescribing advice and policies.

The use of prophylactic antibiotics has been studied in the case of leg ulcers (Alinovi et al, 1986) where it was shown that there were no difference in either healing rate or bacterial flora. The conclusion was that changes in bacterial flora were due to improvement in the general condition of the wound, rather than the therapy.

There is a body of opinion, however, that advocates using antibiotic prophylaxis where *Streptococcus* Group A has been detected because of the possible risk of serious infection, although there is no general agreement. There is similar lack of agreement about whether or not to treat with antibiotics in the case of *Pseudomonas aeruginosa*, although there is evidence that it may be possible to eradicate this organism with the use of a hydrocolloid dressing (Gilchrist and Reed, 1989).

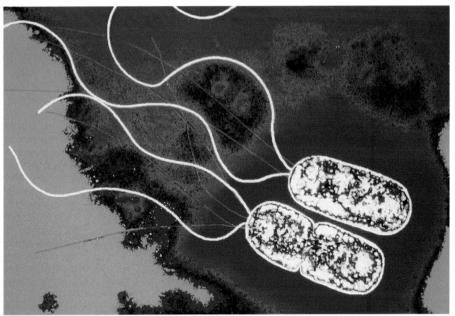

Pseudomonas aeruginosa

Use of antiseptics

The use of antiseptics in chronic wound care continues to be an issue of considerable controversy. In addition to the evidence that chronic wounds do not have to be sterile to heal, there is evidence that wound fluid contains cells and chemicals that are actually beneficial to the wound, such as antibacterial proteins and live white cells, that act as powerful weapons against infection (Hohn et al, 1977a; 1977b). This has led to the realisation that frequent repeated washing of the wound surface may be undesirable and that wounds will heal more efficiently if they are left undisturbed for as long as possible.

Some clinicians feel that the application of an antiseptic may in itself be harmful. 'All antiseptics in normal clinical concentrations are toxic to wound cells *in vitro,* and they have been shown to be destructive of normal tissue as well. Their ability to kill bacteria is compromised in the presence of blood, wound exudate or tissue so that it is unlikely that antiseptics can effectively kill bacteria that are established in tissue' (Rodeheaver, 1990).

Others, however, have reported iodine to be relatively innocuous in terms of toxicity and have also reported that using a derivative of this can be effective when treating chronic wounds (Gilchrist, 1997).

Interpreting the literature is very difficult, as many of the studies have been carried out on animal models, which generally have none of the concurrent factors predisposing them to infection which are found in human with chronic wounds. Neither do most include occlusion as part of the protocol, therefore allowing a scab to form and providing protection for the cells underneath.

The use of iodine in wound care has been reviewed recently (Gilchrist, 1997; Lawrence, 1998). Although there is no evidence that it is harmful to wound healing, there is still a lack of evidence that is promotes it (Welch, 1991). Current interest revolves around the possibility that it may have some other useful bioactivity besides its ability to kill bacteria.

As there is no evidence that bacteria need to be removed from non-infected chronic wounds, and a strong likelihood that toxic chemicals may cause further harm, it would seem that the best solutions for wound care at present are normal saline or tap water. Studies on acute traumatic wounds, where the presence of contamination is more likely to lead to increased wound infection, has shown that the rate of infection is not increased when unsterile tap water is routinely used (Angeras et al, 1992; Riyat and Quintun, 1997). Our own clinical experience using a large bucket of water for wound care in a leg ulcer clinic suggests that the routine use of antiseptics is unnecessary. Tap water has also been used for cleaning pin sites in orthopaedic patients (Brereton, 1998).

Summary

Wound infection is one of the most common hospital-acquired infections in the UK (Emmerson et al, 1996) and it is a problem which causes considerable patient discomfort and undoubtedly contributes to a reduction in healing rates.

Once correctly identified, the principles of treatment are reasonably straightforward: removal or alleviation of known risk factors; proper drainage; the removal of all dead or devitalised tissue; appropriate use of systemic antibiotics; and, possibly the single most important factor which is often overlooked, restoration of an adequate blood supply.

Of lesser importance is the choice of a dressing and, although there is some evidence that occlusion may help to reduce wound infection (Gilchrist and Hutchinson, 1990; Hutchinson and Lawrence, 1991), the treatment of a patient with a wound infection should focus on the whole patient and not just on the hole in their skin.

References

Alinovi, A. et al (1986) Systemic administration of antibiotics in the management of venous ulcers. *Journal of the American Academy of Dermatology*; 15: 2, 186–191.

Angeras, M.H. et al (1992) Comparison between sterile saline and tap water for the cleaning of acute traumatic soft tissue wounds. *European Journal of Surgery*; 158: 33, 347–350.

Blair, S. et al (1988) Do dressings influence the healing of chronic venous ulcers? *Phlebology*; 3: 129–134.

Brereton, V. (1998) Pin-site care and the rate of local infection. *Journal of Wound Care*; 7: 1, 42–44.

Burke, J. (1980) The physiology of wound infection. In: Hunt, T. (ed.) *Wound Healing and Wound Infection*. New York: Appleton-Century-Crofts.

Cruse, P., Foord, R. (1980) The epidemiology of wound infection: a 10-year prospective study of 62,939 wounds. *Surgical Clinics of North America*; 60: 27–40.

Cullum, N, Roe, B. (eds) (1995) *Leg Ulcers: Nursing Management*. Harrow: Scutari Press.

Cutting, K., Harding, K. (1994) Criteria for identifying wound infection. *Journal of Wound Care*; 3: 4, 198–201.

Drug and Therapeutics Bulletin (1991) Local applications to wounds: 1. Cleansers, antibacterials, debriders. *Drug and Therapeutics Bulletin*; 29: 24, 93–95.

Emmerson, A. et al (1996) The Second National Prevalence Survey of Infection in Hospitals – overview of the results. *Journal of Hospital Infection*; 32: 175–190.

Eriksson, G. et al (1994) The clinical significance of bacterial growth in leg ulcers. *Scandinavian Journal of Infectious Diseases*; 16: 175–180.

Finegold, S. (1982) Pathogenic anaerobes. *Archives of Internal Medicine*; 142: 1988–1992.

Gilchrist, B. (1993) Wound infection in the elderly. *Journal of Geriatric Dermatology*; 1: 3, 130–131.

Gilchrist, B. (1996) Sampling bacterial flora: a review of the literature. *Journal of Wound Care*; 5: 8, 386–388.

Gilchrist, B. (1997) Should iodine be reconsidered in wound management? *Journal of Wound Care*; 6: 3, 148–150.

Gilchrist, B., Hutchinson, J. (1990) Does occlusion lead to infection? *Nursing Times*; 86: 15, 70–71.

Gilchrist, B., Reed C. (1989) The bacteriology of chronic venous ulcers treated with occlusive hydrocolloid dressings. *British Journal of Dermatology*; 121: 337–344.

Hansson, C. et al (1995) The microbial flora in venous leg ulcers without clinical signs of infection. *Acta Dermatologica Venereologica* (Stockholm); 75: 24–30.

Heggers, J.P. (1998) Defining infection in chronic wounds: methodology. *Journal of Wound Care*; 7: 9, 452–456.

Hohn, D. et al (1977a) Antimicrobial systems of the surgical wound: 1. A comparison of oxidative metabolism and microbiocidal capacity of phagocytes from wounds and from peripheral blood. *American Journal of Surgery*; 133: 597–600.

Hohn, D. et al (1977b) Antimicrobial systems of the surgical wound: 2. Detection of antimicrobial protein in cell-free wound fluid. *American Journal of Surgery*; 133: 601–606.

Hutchinson, J. (1992) Influence of occlusive dressings on wound microbiology: interim results of a multi-centre clinical trial of an occlusive hydrocolloid dressing. In: Harding, K. et al (eds) *Proceedings of the First European Conference on Advances in Wound Management*. London: Macmillan.

Hutchinson, J., Lawrence, J. (1991) Wound infection under occlusive dressings. *Journal of Hospital Infection*; 17: 83–94.

Lancet (1990) Management of smelly tumours. (editorial). *Lancet*; 335: 141–142.

Lauria, D.B. (1985) Factors predisposing to clinical infections of the skin. In: Maibach, H.I., Hildick-Smith, G. (eds) *Skin Bacteria and Their Role in Infection*. New York: McGraw Hill.

Lawrence, J.C. (1998) The use of iodine as an antiseptic agent. *Journal of Wound Care*; 7: 8, 421–425.

Leaper, D. (1995) Risk factors for surgical infection. *Journal of Hospital Infection*; 30 (supplement), 127–139.

Mertz, P., Eaglestein, W. (1984) The effect of a semi-occlusive dressing on the microbial population in superficial wounds. *Archives of Surgery*; 119: 287–289.

Mishriki, S. et al (1990) Factors affecting the incidence of postoperative wound infection. *Journal of Hospital Infection*; 16: 223–230.

Neal, M. (1994) Necrotising infections. *Nursing Times*; 90: 41, 53–59.

Neal, M. (1998) Necrotising fasciitis. *Journal of Wound Care*; 8: 1, 18–19.

Riyat, M., Quintun, D. (1997) Tap water as a wound cleansing agent in accident and emergency. *Journal of Accident and Emergency Medicine*; 14: 165–166.

Robson, M. (1991) Plastic surgery. In: Heggers, J., Robson, M. (eds) *Quantitative Bacteriology: Its Role in the Arnamentarium of the Surgeon*. Florida: CRC Press.

Robson, M. et al (1990) Wound healing alterations caused by infection. *Clinics in Plastic Surgery*; 17: 3, 485–492.

Rodeheaver, G. (1990) Influence of antiseptics on wound healing. In: Alexander, J.W., Thompson, P.D., Hutchinson, J.J. (eds) *International Forum on Wound Microbiology*. Princeton: Excerpta Medica.

Schneider, M. et al (1983) Quantitative assessment of bacterial invasion of chronic ulcers. *American Journal of Surgery*; 145: 260–262.

Selwyn, S. (1981) The topical treatment of skin infections. In: Maibach, H., Aly, R. (eds) *Skin Microbiology: Relevance to Clinical Infection*. New York: Springer Verlag.

Spencer, R. (1993) National prevalence survey of hospital acquired infections: definitions. *Journal of Hospital Infection*; 24: 69–76.

Stotts, N. (1995) Determination of bacterial burden in wounds. *Advances in Wound Care*; 8: 8, 46–52.

Swann, A. (1985) Bacterial infection. *Care Science and Practice*; 1: 14–17

Thompson, P., Smith, D. (1994) What is infection? In Kerstein, M. (ed.) A symposium: wound infection and occlusion – separating fact from fiction. *American Journal of Surgery*; 167: (1A) (supplement), S7-S11.

Tobin, G, (1984) Closure of contaminated wounds. *Surgical Clinics of North America*; 64: 4, 639–652.

Trengove, N.J. et al (1996) Qualitative bacteriology and leg ulcer healing. *Journal of Wound Care*; 5: 6, 277–280.

Vowden, K.R. (1996) Hand-held Doppler assessment for peripheral arterial disease. *Journal of Wound Care*; 6: 3, 125–128.

Welch, J.S. (1991) Letter. *Ostomy and Wound Management*; 35: 28–29.

10 Nutrition in wound healing

David Gray
Pam Cooper

Key points

▶ The importance of nutrition and its role in wound healing is often overlooked by health care professionals

▶ Protein depletion can cause delays in wound healing

▶ An accurate assessment should be undertaken to identify patients at risk from inadequate nutrition

Introduction

While many other parts of this book may refer to advances in technology, the role of nutrition in the healing of wounds and the promotion of health is a low priority for many in health care. In this chapter we aim, first, to identify the role of macro/micronutrients and minerals in the healing of wounds and, second, to suggest methods of nutritional assessment.

Macronutrients

Carbohydrates

As the body attempts to heal so its metabolic rate increases and subsequently the demand for carbohydrates. Cellular activity, such as the metabolism of leukocytes and fibroblasts, is fuelled by adenosine triphosphate which is derived from glucose. Carbohydrates are broken down to provide glucose (Casey, 1998; Lewis and Harding, 1993).

Where this important source of energy is depleted the body breaks down protein to provide amino acids which are broken down to provide the glucose required for cellular activity (Lewis and Harding, 1993; Collins, 1996).

Proteins

Where a wound is present so the body's demand for protein is increased, the main protein synthesised during healing is collagen (Casey, 1998) In the event of sepsis or stress the requirement for protein can rise. It is also suggested that even short spells of protein depletion can in some wounds can result in poor clinical outcomes (Wallace, 1992).

Proteins are required for the inflammatory phase and the development of granulation tissue (Lewis and Harding, 1993; Wallace, 1992; McLaren, 1992). Protein depletion can lead to the prolonging of the inflammatory phase, poor collagen synthesis and disrupted wound remodelling (Lewis and Harding, 1993; Collins, 1996; McLaren, 1992).

If protein depletion is severe then this can result in the development of oedema owing to hypoalbuminaemia. Both human and animal studies have suggested that protein depletion can effect the rate and quality of healing (McLaren, 1992; Garrow and James, 1993; Wilkinson and Hawke, 1999).

Fats

Essential fatty acids must be provided by the diet as they cannot be synthesised. The role of fatty acids is not clearly understood but as they are heavily involved in the synthesis of new cells any depletion may affect repair (Lewis and Harding, 1993; Collins, 1996; McLaren, 1992).

Vitamins

Vitamins have a role to play as co-factors in a wide range of metabolic and physiological functions involved in wound healing (Lewis and Harding, 1993).

Vitamin C

Vitamin C plays an important part in the synthesis of collagen; it is required in the formation of bonds between strands of collagen fibre. This activity provides extra strength and stability to the collagen. Injury, stress and sepsis increase the body's requirement for vitamin C, but there is no evidence to suggest that providing megadoses of the vitamin improves clinical outcomes (Casey, 1998; Lewis and Harding, 1993; McLaren, 1992).

Vitamin C deficiency could lead to a slower healing rate and the increased risk of surgical wound dehiscence (Lewis and Harding, 1993: McLaren, 1992).

Vitamin K

Vitamin K has a role to play in the formation of thrombin and deficiency could lead to the development of a haematoma (Garrow and James, 1993).

11 Choosing the right dressing

Sylvie Hampton

Key points

▶ The success of any dressing results from careful selection related to the individual patient

▶ Dressings can be used to aid debridement, remove excess exudate, control bleeding and protect a wound

▶ All dressings should provide the optimum wound healing environment

▶ Each stage of wound healing will require a specific dressing

Introduction

Application of any wound dressing is of little value unless all factors that may delay wound healing have been assessed and problems addressed. Torrance (1983) has stated: 'Nursing interventions have tended to focus on the wound itself, but a more holistic approach is important. Systemic factors may be more important than the local wound care.' Therefore good assessment is the single most important part of wound healing.

Very few dressings physically interact with the wound. Dressings will only provide an optimum wound healing environment when chosen to address specific requirements.

In cost-effectiveness terms, a dressing that promotes rapid healing reduces cost and improves quality of life. Therefore, even if it is more expensive then another less effective dressing, it is cost-effective.

This chapter will provide the nurse with information about the function and selection of dressings.

Using dressings to aid wound debridement

Debridement is the surgical removal of macerated, devitalised or contaminated tissue by various means.

Sharp surgical debridement

The most rapid and effective method of debridement is sharp or surgical, where necrotic tissue is dissected from viable tissue by use of sterile scissors or scalpel. This may be performed at the bedside by an experienced practitioner (Hampton, 1997a; Hoffman, 1996). If performed by an inexperienced practitioner this procedure could be dangerous, as connective tissue can have the appearance of slough so there is a potential for tendons and/or ligaments to be accidentally severed (Hampton, 1997a).

Surgical debridement requires knowledge of underlying structures, an understanding of wound assessment, and the experience to decide when debridement should not be performed (Hampton, 1997a).

Certain necrotic wounds should not be debrided (Hampton, 1997a; Hoffman, 1996):

▶ ischaemic feet

▶ malignant wounds that are likely to bleed

▶ wounds that may have other structures close to the surface

Enzymatic debridement

Streptokinase and streptodornase is a combination of enzymes traditionally used to promote debridement of necrotic wounds. Streptokinase is an anti-thrombolytic which acts directly on a substrate of fibrin, breaks down fibrin and fibrinogen and facilitates wound debridement (Flanagan, 1997). It activates a fibrinolytic enzyme in human serum which breaks up thrombi (Martin, 1996). Streptodornase liquefies the viscous nucleoprotein of dead cells or pus. The joint action of the two enzymes rehydrates the hard necrotic material in a wound and allows the secondary dressing and/or irrigation to remove the liquefied matter.

There are limitations to the use of these agents which are outlined in Box 1 below.

▶ Streptokinase and streptodornase poured directly on to a wound is unlikely to remain in the required position

▶ Changing dressings twice daily is difficult to achieve on very busy wards

▶ The cost of streptokinase and streptodornase is prohibitive, particularly when there is a lack of evidence to suggest that it is more effective than other debriding agents (Martin, 1996)

▶ Streptokinase and streptodornase is not effective when used on dehydrated and hard eschar (Flanagan, 1997)

Box 1 Potential problems associated with use of enzymatic dressings

---

Hydrogel and hydrocolloid debridement

Gels and hydrocolloid dressings are commonly used to aid debridement. These are covered later in this chapter.

Using dressings to treat symptoms

Pain

Wounds that are painful need dressings that will gently 'bathe' nerve endings. Hydrogels, hydrocolloids or sheet gels will all achieve this. Venous ulcers are often painful, but this can be resolved within a few hours by the application of a dressing and compression bandage (Franks et al, 1995) Analgesia is an option that should be considered if the pain cannot be controlled with a dressing and is sometimes required as a short-term method of reducing the pain while the dressing completes its role in pain control.

Some hydrophilic dressings such as sugar paste or a cadexamer that exert an osmotic 'pull' on the wound bed are likely to increase pain (Hampton, 1997b).

Odour

Odour in a wound can be an indication of bacteria (Flanagan, 1997). Reduce the colonisation and odour will disappear. Gram-negative bacteria such as pseudomonas can be malodorous and distressing for the patient and carers. Treatment over three days with silver sulphadiazine cream can reduce colonisation and the amount of dressing changes required (Dealey, 1994).

Wounds colonised by *Staphylococcus aureus* or streptococcus may benefit from a cadexamer paste or a non-adherent povidone-iodine dressing (Gilchrist, 1997). Carbon dressings adsorb odour. Some contain silver which destroys bacteria (Flanagan, 1997). This promotes healing while reducing odour.

Exudate

A general rule of thumb in selecting a dressing is to maintain a moist environment at the wound bed while removing excess exudate to prevent maceration (Winter, 1962; Dyson, 1988; Turner, 1985; Miller, 1994).

Exudate, malodour and maceration of peri-wound areas may be problematic as each can cause distress for the patient. However, exudate also contains growth factors that promote tissue regeneration (Kreig and Eming, 1997).

Several factors can combine to increase the amount of exudate, such as:

▶ hydrostatic pressure (Nelson, 1996a; Nelson, 1996b; Thomas, 1997)

▶ wound infection/colonisation (Flanagan, 1997; Gottrup, 1997; Harding, 1997)

▶ wound type (Thomas, 1997). For example, because of their particular disease mechanism, venous ulcers are likely to produce higher levels of exudate than arterial ulcers which have poor blood supply. Lymphatic drainage problems can occur following surgery for cancer and this can increase exudate (Gottrup, 1997)

If colonisation is reduced exudate will decrease. Hydrostatic pressure is also an important element in exudate production. Capillary pressure, for example, can be high in the case of hypertension in venous disease (Thomas, 1997). This expands the veins and pushes fluid into the wound bed. Exudate will reduce when pressure is applied by using compression bandages or a dressing that forms a seal around the wound such as a hydrocolloid (Harding, 1997).

Another useful way of keeping the wound moist but free from harmful exudate is through vacuum-assisted closure.

Bleeding

Fungating wounds bleed easily. Some alginates have haemostatic properties (*British National Formulary*, 1991) and exchange calcium ions for sodium ions in the wound bed. Calcium initiates the clotting cascade (Thomas, 1992).

Infection/colonisation

If a wound has obvious signs of infection then systemic antibiotic treatment must be considered, as infected wounds will not heal.

Antiseptics and disinfectants

Silver

Several dressings contain silver and probably the most widely used of these is silver sulphadiazine cream. This cream is particularly useful in the treatment of Gram-negative infections such as pseudomonas (*British National Formulary*, 1991).

Because of the slow release of silver ions over a period of up to seven days, bacteria on the wound surface can be destroyed using film dressings containing silver (Gilchrist, 1996).

Some silver dressings also contain carbon to reduce wound odour. These should be used as primary dressings to ensure the silver effectively kills bacteria, but they are sometimes used, mistakenly, as secondary dressings to eliminate odour. This is not cost-effective.

Iodine

There is not yet any proven resistance to iodine (Leelaporn et al, 1994; Hampton, 1997c) and Goldheim, (1993) reports that povidone-iodine will not affect wound healing adversely. Nevertheless, iodine is rapidly deactivated in the presence of pus and may, therefore, have limited use as an anti-microbial (Leaper, 1987).

There are iodine-based cadexamer dressings which have the ability to absorb exudate in exchange for iodine. This allows a slower release of iodine into the wound, thereby extending antiseptic activity (Flanagan, 1997). A dressing containing povidone-iodine, is useful in treating superficial colonised wounds.

Hypochlorites

Hypochlorites are no longer widely used because:

▶ the antimicrobial properties are quickly deactivated in the presence of pus (Leaper, 1988; Dealey, 1994)

▶ application and removal is painful (Dealey, 1994)

▶ they may delay wound healing by destroying cells and capillaries (Leaper; 1988. Dealey, 1994)

Hydrogen peroxide

Hydrogen peroxide is a weak antiseptic which breaks down on contact with the wound to liberate oxygen and water (Ferguson, 1993). It is thought that the oxygen release, which causes foaming, is the action that cleanses the wound. However, there are dangers in using hydrogen peroxide, particularly in cavity wounds as the liberation of oxygen in the wound bed can cause air emboli to enter the bloodstream (Bassan et al, 1982).

Dressing selection

Dressing selection relies on the skilful observation of the assessing nurse. Appropriate selection will lead to provision of the optimum wound healing environment (Table 1).

Moisture	A moist wound environment will accelerate epidermal migration (Winter, 1962) and dermal repair (Dyson, 1988) (see Figures 1–4)
Thermal insulation	A drop in temperature below 37° delays mitotic activity for up to four hours (Torrance, 1986; Lock, 1979; Myers, 1982)
Highly absorptive	Excess exudate can macerate healthy tissue surrounding the wound
Impermeable to bacteria	Protection of the wound against bacterial contamination
	'Strike-through' of exudate allows passage for bacteria into and out of the wound (Dealey, 1994; Hallett and Hampton, 1999)
Free of contaminants	Foreign bodies can act as foci for infection (Hallett and Hampton, 1999)
Non-adherent	Adherent dressings may cause trauma to new tissue. Capillaries can grow through gauze and will be torn when the gauze is removed
Non toxic	Laboratory evidence has shown that some antiseptics and hypochlorites are toxic to certain cells. This has not been demonstrated in human studies (Flanagan, 1997; Leaper, 1988; Goldheim, 1993; Ferguson, 1993; Sleigh and Linter, 1985; Morgan, 1992)

Table 1 Dressing requirements for providing an optimum wound healing environment (Turner, 1985)

Histology slides demonstrating the benefits of moist wound healing (Dyson et al 1988)

Figure 1 Histology section of a dry wound in porcine skin after five days of healing

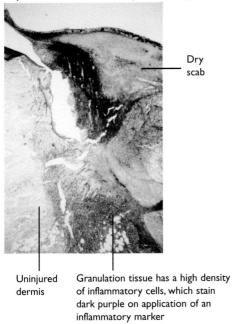

Dry scab

Uninjured dermis

Granulation tissue has a high density of inflammatory cells, which stain dark purple on application of an inflammatory marker

Figure 2 Histology section of a dry wound in porcine skin after seven days of healing

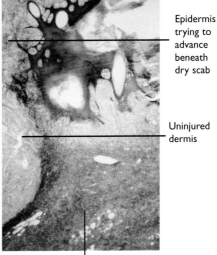

Epidermis trying to advance beneath dry scab

Uninjured dermis

Granulation tissue still has a high density of inflammatory cells

Figure 3 Histology section of a moist wound in porcine skin after five days of healing

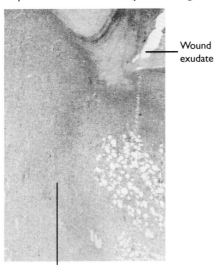

Wound exudate

Granulation tissue, consisting mostly of proliferative cells

Figure 4 Histology section of a moist wound in porcine skin after seven days of healing

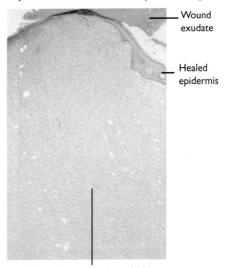

Wound exudate

Healed epidermis

Granulation tissue has a high density of proliferative cells

Dressings that create an optimum wound environment

Alginates

Alginates were first used in the 1940s (Thomas and Loveless, 1992). They are made from seaweed and can be composed of galuronic and mannuronic acid, with the proportions of these determining the gel forming properties of the final fibre (Williams, 1994). High galuronic acid alginates produce firmer gels (Thomas and Loveless, 1992). This gives the gelled fibres strength and retains the shape of the dressing in the wound bed, enabling it to be lifted out in one piece.

The alginates high in mannuronic acid are weaker and the gel from these can be rinsed out of a wound with normal saline. Some alginates encourage the clotting cascade within a bleeding wound.

Alginates are best used in moderate to highly exuding wounds (Miller and Dyson, 1996). If the wound bed is too dry the alginate will not gel and will adhere to the wound bed.

An alternative to alginate dressings is a hydrofibre sheet or ribbon. This dressing retains a high quantity of water without releasing it, thereby forming a thick conformable gel (Flanagan, 1997).

Film dressings

Semi-permeable films play an important role in wound care both as primary and secondary dressings. Films are made of clear polyurethane coated with an adhesive. Owing to their highly elastomeric and extensible properties, these dressings are conformable and resistant to shear and tear. Films will prevent bacterial colonisation but do not absorb exudate. Film dressings are generally vapour-permeable and allow fluid to evaporate while keeping the wound moist (Flanagan, 1997).

Foams

A foam is a term used to describe a dressing made using advanced polymer technology. They are non-adherent, can absorb large amounts of exudate and can also be used as secondary dressings. Hydropolymer dressings incorporate a wicking layer and a skin-friendly adhesive. This can be released by wiping the adhesive edge with water and then reapplied shortly afterwards. The hydropolymer swells into the wound bed as exudate is absorbed. The exudate then evaporates out of the back of the dressing.

Hydrocellular polyurethane dressings can absorb several times their own weight in exudate. These have a trilaminate structure comprised of a non-adherent wound contact layer, a highly absorbent centre and an outer layer.

Other foams made of absorbent polyurethane foam are indicated for light to moderately exudating open wounds. Exudate is absorbed into the foam and becomes visible at the edge of the dressing once it is saturated but will not pass through the outer layer.

Hydrocolloids

Hydrocolloids consist of a mixture of pectins, gelatines, sodium carboxymethylcellulose and elastomers.

Hydrocolloids create an environment that encourages autolysis to debride wounds that are sloughy or necrotic (Cherry and Ryan, 1985; Dealey, 1993). There is also evidence that hydrocolloids reduce pain in wounds (Rousseau, 1991).

Hydrocolloids are occlusive thus providing a hypoxic environment which is thought to encourage angiogenesis in acute wounds (Cherry and Ryan, 1985). As the hydrocolloid mixes with exudate, it produces a yellow gel with a characteristic odour which the patient should be told about (Flanagan, 1997). Care should be taken to ensure that the correct size of dressing is applied, that is, one large enough to cover the wound with an overlap of at least 2cm.

These dressings are waterproof, enabling the patient bath or shower without removing the dressing.

Hydrogels

Hydrogels come in two basic forms, sheets and gels. The sheets comprise polysaccharide agarose, cross-linked with polyacrylamide. Hydrogel sheets are used for shallow wounds (Flanagan, 1997) such as burns, fungating lesions, skin graft donor sites or low-exuding wounds. The gels are suitable for cavities and are effective for desloughing and debriding wounds (Bale, 1997).

Gels have a high water content which aids the rehydration of hard eschar and promotes autolysis in necrotic wounds. They can be used in cavity or shallow wounds and are effective at desloughing and debriding (Flanagan, 1997). A secondary dressing is needed to keep the gel moist and *in situ* (Hampton, 1998a).

A problem that may occur with use of a hydrogel and secondary dressing is maceration and excoriation of the peri-wound areas from leakage of the gel and exudate. This can be addressed through the use of a protective barrier film (Hampton, 1998c).

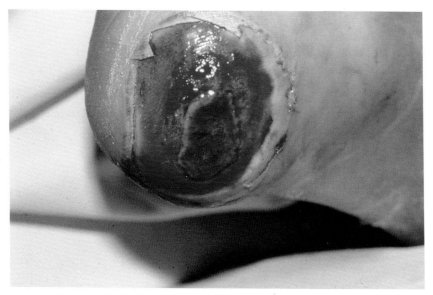

A partially debrided necrotic heel ulcer

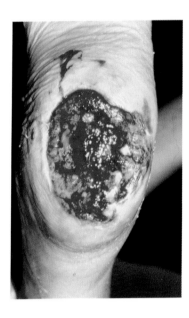

A fully debrided necrotic heel ulcer, showing healthy granulation tissue

Vacuum-assisted closure

Vacuum-assisted closure is a system that creates a hypoxic environment within the wound bed in which aerobic bacteria cannot survive. This environment forces the microcirculation to regenerate rapidly and produce large amounts of capillaries. At the same time, the negative pressure will 'pull' blood into the wound bed bringing with it growth factors and macrophages to an area depleted in bacterial contamination. This leaves large reserves of oxygen as energy for tissue regeneration.

The negative pressure also removes slough and loose necrotic material from the wound bed leaving it clean with an excellent blood supply. This encourages the proliferation of granulation tissue (Morykwas and Louis, 1993) and ensures that white blood cells are supplied with necessary oxygen through the bloodstream, while anaerobic bacteria in the wound bed die.

Wound colonisation has been found to reduce 1,000 times in four days in wounds treated with vacuum-assisted closure therapy (Collier, 1997).

Wound type	Basic requirements	Suitable dressings/treatment
Black (hard eschar)	Rehydration Debridement	Enzymatic treatment Hydrogels Hydrocolloids Larvae therapy Sharp debridement
Soft black Yellow	Removal	Cadexamer iodine Hydrogels Hydrocolloids Vacuum assisted closure
Green/malodorous	Reducing infection/colonisation	Charcoal dressing incorporating silver Film dressing incorporating silver (superficial wounds) Povodine-iodine/iodine Silver sulphadiazine cream Sugar paste Vacuum assisted closure
Clinical infection	Treat infection and manage exudate and odour	Cadexamer iodine Charcoal dressing incorporating silver Film dressing incorporating silver (superficial wounds) Povidone-iodine Silver sulphadiazine cream Sugar paste Vacuum assisted closure
Granulating	Create moist environment and manage exudate	Alginates Foams Semi-permeable films (superficial wounds) Hydrocolloids Non-adherent dressings of any type Vacuum assisted closure (cavity wounds) Wound contact layers
Epithelialising	Create moist environment	Semi-permeable films Foams Thin hydrocolloids Non-adherent dressings Non-adherent hydropolymer

Table 2 Which dressing for which wound

Conclusion

Selection of the appropriate dressing for the individual wound relies on holistic assessment of the patient. Provision of the optimum wound-healing environment is essential; choice of dressings is a skill acquired through education and experience. Debridement of necrotic wounds, reduction of exudate, colonisation, malodour and pain can be achieved through a knowledge of dressings and their interactions.

The future of wound care is not with *managing* wounds but in *treating* wounds and this needs to be developed in the context of the multidisciplinary team. Ultimately, the nurse is accountable to the patient and should be aware of current dressings and new developments to ensure that the patient receives the highest standard of care.

References

Bale, S. (1997) A guide to wound debridement. *Journal of Wound Care*; 6: 4, 179–182.

Bassan, M. et al (1982). Near fatal systemic oxygen embolism due to irrigation with hydrogen peroxide. *Postgraduate Medical Journal*; 58: 448–450.

British Medical Association and the Pharmaceutical Society of Great Britain. *British National Formulary (No. 22)*. London: BMA/PSGB.

Cherry, G.W., Ryan, T.J. (1985) Enhanced wound angiogenesis with a new hydrocolloid dressing. *Royal Society of Medicine International Congress and Symposium Series*; 88: 5–14.

Collier, M. (1997) Know how: a guide to vacuum-assisted closure. *Nursing Times* (supplement); January 1997.

Dealey, C. (1994) *The Care of Wounds*. Oxford: Blackwell Science.

Dealey, C. (1993) The role of hydrocolloids in wound management. *British Journal of Nursing*; 2: 7, 358–365.

Dyson, M. et al (1988). Comparison of the effects of moist and dry conditions on dermal repair. *Journal of Investigative Dermatology*; 91: 5, 435–439.

Ferguson, A. (1993) Wound infection: the role of antiseptics. *Accident and Emergency Nursing*; 1: 79–86.

Flanagan, M. (1997) *Wound Management*. Edinburgh: Churchill Livingstone.

Franks, P.J. et al (1995) Risk factors for leg ulcer recurrence: a randomised trial of two types of compression stocking. *Age and Aging*; 24: 490–494.

Gilchrist, B. (1996) *Silver in Infection Control* (poster presentation). Tissue Viability Conference, Derby.

Gilchrist, B. (1997) Should iodine be reconsidered in wound management? *Journal of Wound Care*; 6: 3, 148–150.

Goldheim, P. (1993) An appraisal of povidone–iodine and wound healing. *Postgraduate Medical Journal*; (Supplement 3): S98–S105.

Gottrup, F. (1997) Is exudate a clinical problem? A surgeon's perspective. In: *Management of Wound Exudate.* Cherry, C., Harding, K. (eds) *Proceedings of Joint Meeting of EWMA and ETRS.* London: Churchill Communications.

Hallett, A., Hampton, S. (1999). *Wound Dressings.* Huntingdon: Wound Care Society.

Hampton, S. (1997a) Sharp debridement. *Journal of Wound Care*; 6: 3, 151.

Hampton S (1997b) Wound assessment. *Professional Nurse Study Supplement*; 12: 12, S5–S7.

Hampton, S. (1997c) Germ warfare. *Nursing Times*; 93: 40, 74–79.

Hampton, S. (1997c) *Treatment of Macerated and Excoriated Peri-Wound Area with No-Sting Barrier Film.* Presented in poster form at European Wound Management Conference, Harrogate.

Hampton, S. (1998a) Dressing selection. *Nursing Scotland.*

Hampton, S. (1998b) Film subjects win the day. *Nursing Times*; 94: 24, 80–82.

Hansson, C. et al Repeated treatment with lidocaine/prilocaine cream (EMLA) as a topical anaesthetic for the cleansing of venous leg ulcers: a controlled study. *Acta Dermatologica Venerealogica* (Stockholm); 73: 231–233.

Harding, K. (1997) Is exudate a clinical problem? A specialist physician's perspective. In: (eds) *Management of Wound Exudate:* Cherry, C., Harding, K. (eds) *Proceedings of Joint Meeting of EWMA and ETRS.* London: Churchill Communications.

Hoffman, D. (1996) Know how: a guide to wound debridement. *Nursing Times (supplement)*; 92: 32, 22–23.

Kreig, T., Eming, A.S. (1997) Is exudate a clinical problem? A dermatologists perspective. In: (eds) Cherry, G., Harding, K. *Management of Wound Exudate: Proceedings of Joint Meeting of EWMA and ETRS.* London: Churchill Communications.

Kristofferson, A. (1998) Lidocaine-prilocaine cream (EMLA) as a topical anaesthetic for the cleansing of leg ulcers: the effect of length of application time. *European Journal of Dermatology*; 8: 4, 245–247.

Leaper, D. (1987) Antiseptic solutions. *Nursing Times Community Outlook* (supplement); 83; 8, 30–34.

Leaper, D. (1988) Antiseptic toxicity in open wounds. *Nursing Times*; 84: 25, 77–79.

Leelaporn, A. et al (1994) Multidrug resistance to antiseptics and disinfectants in coagulase-negative staphylococci. *Journal of Medical Biology*; 40: 214–230.

Lock, (1979) The effects of temperature on mitotic activities at the edge of experimental wounds. *Proceedings of Symposium on Wound Healing, Espo, Finland.* Chatham, Kent: Lock Laboratories Research.

Martin, S.J. (1996) Enzymatic debridement for necrotic wounds. *Journal of Wound Care*; 5: 7, 310–311.

Miller, M., Dyson, M. (1996) *Principles of Wound Care.* London: Macmillan Magazines.

Miller, M. (1994) The ideal wound environment. *Nursing Times*; 90: 45, 62–68.

Morykwas, M.J., Louis, C. (1993) Use of negative pressure to increase the rate of granulation tissue formation in chronic open wounds. *Proceedings of the Annual Meeting Federation of American Societies for Experimental Biology* (March 28 – April 1). New Orleans: Federation of American Societies for Experimental Biology.

Morgan, D. (1997) Myiasis: the rise and fall of maggot therapy. *Journal of Tissue Viability*; 5: 2, 43–51.

Myers, J.A. (1982) Modern plastic surgical dressings. *Health Society Service Journal*; 4: 336–337.

Nelson, E.A. (1996a) Compression bandaging in the treatment of venous leg ulcers. *Journal of Wound Care*; 5: 9, 415–418.

Nelson, A. (1996b) Compression bandaging in the treatment of leg ulcers. *Journal of Wound Care*; 5: 9, 415–418.

Parker, G.E. (1994) Hungry healers. *Nursing Times*; 90: 24, 55–58.

Raman, A. et al (1995) Antimicrobial effects of tea-tree oil and its major components on *staphylococcus aureus*, *S. epidermis* and *Propionibacterium acnes*. *Letter to Applied Microbiology*; 21: 4, 242–245.

Rousseau, P. (1991) Comparison of the various physiochemical properties of various hydrocolloid dressings. *Wounds*; 3: 1, 43–48.

Rund, C.R.(1996) Non-conventional topical therapies for wound care. *Ostomy Wound Management*; 42: 5, 18–20.

Thomas, S. (1992) Alginates. *Journal of Wound Care*; 1: 1, 29–32.

Thomas, S. (1997) Exudate: who needs it? In: Cherry, C., Harding, K. (eds) *Management of Wound Exudate*: *Proceedings of Joint Meeting of EWMA and ETRS*. London: Churchill Communications.

Thomas, S., Loveless, P. (1991) A comparative study of the properties of six hydrocolloid dressings. *Pharmaceutical Journal*; 247: 672–675.

Thomas, S., Loveless, P. (1992) Observations on the fluid handling properties of alginate dressings. *Pharmaceutical Journal*; 248: 850–851.

Thomas, S. et al (1996) Using larvae in modern wound management. *Journal of Wound Care*; 5: 2, 60–69.

Torrance, C. (1983) *Pressure Sores: Aetiology, Treatment and Prevention*. London: Croom Helm.

Torrance, C. (1986) The physiology of wound healing. *Nursing*; 5: 162–166.

Turner, T.D. (1985) Which dressing and why? In: Westaby, S. (ed.) *Wound Care*. London: Heinemann.

Williams, C. (1994) Kaltostat. *British Journal of Nursing*; 3: 18.

Winter, G.D. (1962) Formation of the scab and rate of epithelialisation of superficial wounds in the skin of a young domestic pig. *Nature*; 193: 293–294.

12 Larval therapy

Mary Jones

Andrea Andrews

Key points

▶ Larval therapy has been used in wound healing for centuries

▶ Sterile maggots from the *Lucilia sericata* fly are used

▶ Exudate production will increase when maggots are used on a wound

▶ It is imperative that patients are prepared psychologically if therapy is undertaken

Introduction

The use of maggots (larval therapy) to treat wounds is not a new concept, although in early times larval infestation was mostly accidental. Larval therapy is mentioned in the Bible, with Job described as 'clothed with worms' owing to his 'loathsome and painful sores'. Later, Ambroise Paré, considered to be the founder of surgery, refers to the use of maggots in wounds (Paré, 1579).

More recent documentation dating from the 1800s records the successful use of maggots by military surgeon Baron Dominique Larrey to treat wounds during the Napoleonic wars. Larrey recorded his observations of larvae in wounds that were complicated by erysipelas (acute inflammatory disease caused by haemolytic streptococcus), gangrene and tetanus (Larrey, 1832).

Larvae were used by the military throughout the First and Second World Wars, where they were applied to sloughy or necrotic wounds to remove devitalised tissue that prevented healing (McKeever, 1933).

Another military orthopaedic surgeon, Zaccharias, was so impressed by the effect of larvae on traumatic wounds that he said: 'Maggots in a single day would clean a wound much better than any agent we had at our command. I'm sure we saved many lives by their use' (Zaccharias, 1904).

There is a great deal recorded about the use of larvae in treating osteomyelitis and small carcinomas (Bunkis et al, 1985). Although this literature is old, it does not necessarily follow that it is irrelevant.

During the 1950s antibiotics changed the way wounds were managed and the use of larvae declined, although isolated reports about benefits from accidental contamination continued.

Recently, antibiotic-resistant organisms have provided medical practitioners with new challenges. One solution to this problem is larval therapy.

The revival of larval therapy

The Biosurgical Research Unit (BRU), in Bridgend, has perfected a method of producing sterile maggots for use in wound care. The larvae are from the *Lucilia sericata* species of fly, commonly known as the greenbottle because of its metallic green hue.

This species was selected for two reasons: first, the life-cycle of *Lucilia sericata* has been well documented and was successfully used by surgeons in the 1930s (Baer, 1931); second, the larvae of this species produce powerful enzymes which break down only dead tissue (Vistnes, 1981). They do not, as some believe, burrow into healthy tissue.

How the treatment works

When larvae are applied to a wound they are about 2–3mm long. Under favourable conditions they increase rapidly in size during the two to three days they are at the wound site and are approximately 8–10mm in length when removed. They feed head down and tail up and breathe through spiracles in their tails. They break down and liquefy dead tissue rapidly by depositing powerful proteolytic enzymes.

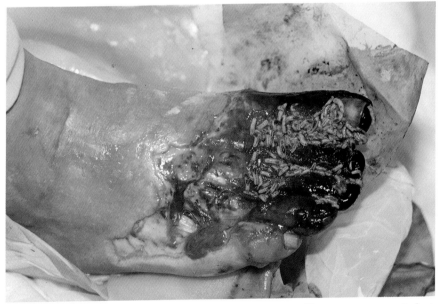

Maggots on a necrotic foot

The larvae then 'suck' the fluid in and digest it. Larvae secrete allantoin and urea (Robinson, 1935), ammonia (Robinson, 1940) and calcium carbonate (Messer and McClellan, 1935). All these agents are claimed to be beneficial for wound healing. Calcium ions are believed to stimulate phagocytosis (Schmidt et al, 1993). If there are any organisms in the devitalised tissue, larvae ingest and destroy them.

The larvae of *Lucilia sericata* are completely ineffective at liquefying intact human tissue and, because they do not bite or tear, do not put any pressure on the wound bed and cannot be felt. But it should be noted that there will always be an increase in exudate production and a distinctive odour. It is important that both practitioners and patients know this will happen, as otherwise the increase in exudate and odour may be misinterpreted as a wound infection. During treatment the wound changes colour to pink/red.

After a period of two to three days, the larvae are easily removed from the wound and should be disposed of by incineration. This ensures they will not enter the food chain. If they did it could have unforeseen consequences, because although the maggots are sterile they have been in contaminated wounds and their outer casing may be contaminated with organisms. The maggots do not have to be incinerated immediately; the life-cycle of the maggots means that there are nine days from the time they are removed from a wound to when they hatch as adult flies (Thomas, 1996).

Producing sterile larvae

Early literature describes numerous ways of fly rearing and egg sterilisation (Weil, 1931). BRU has refined these techniques and developed its own consistent method of egg sterilisation which is subject to numerous quality control checks.

The larvae are bred from a large stock of flies that have been strictly monitored since 1995. The flies themselves are not sterile but socially clean; it is the eggs that undergo sterilisation, rendering them free from contamination before the larvae hatch. After hatching, the larvae are kept for 48 hours to undergo a series of quality control checks before being transferred to sterile containers for dispatch.

Use of larval therapy

Initially, the revived larval therapy was viewed by clinicians as a treatment of last resort. Patients receiving the therapy were often elderly and in poor physical condition. A number of patients therefore died before wound treatment was completed. But although patients' physical condition continued to deteriorate, it was noted that their wounds showed signs of improvement.

Nowadays, as news of the treatment's success has been disseminated, patients are being referred earlier and the treatment is no longer viewed as a last resort. In some instances it is now the second option after surgical intervention has been ruled out. This has resulted in some interesting case histories being published both in the press and on the internet (Jones et al, 1998).

Further research and development is being carried out, particularly on the effect of larval enzymes on granulation tissue formation.

It is recommended that larvae are applied to the wound as soon as possible after delivery, preferably within 12 hours (BRU, 1997). If it is not possible to apply them immediately, it is recommended that the container is stored in a cool, dark place, preferably at a temperature of 8–10°C.

Because maggot therapy is, in effect, a 'living' dressing, there are a few limitations to the patient's lifestyle. While the larvae remain on the wound the patient is advised not to bath or shower as this could drown the maggots.

A helpline is available at BRU to assist practitioners with any related problems.

Larval therapy has a sound basis in the literature and does not appear to have any significant side-effects. It may offer advantages over surgical debridement because no general anaesthetic is needed. However, larval treatment can present practitioners with ethical dilemmas. While it is true that maggots can be applied to almost any wound containing devitalised tissue, not all patients are suitable for the therapy. There is also a danger of turning the treatment into a 'side-show' for clinicians, where the patient may be of secondary importance to the therapy. It is essential to maintain patient focus (UKCC, 1994).

Some patients find the thought of maggots in their wounds unacceptable and they should not be pressured into accepting the therapy. Practitioners must take time to explain the treatment fully. If the patient refuses the treatment, the nurse must ensure alternative treatments are offered. Informed consent must be obtained but this does not necessarily mean written consent or approval from the local ethics committee, unless local policies dictate that these forms of approval are mandatory.

Conclusion

Larval therapy is back in vogue and offers an effective approach to wound debridement and removing bacteria. Specially bred, sterile maggots which liquefy dead tissue using enzymes are now available to treat a range of wounds. Some patients or medical/nursing staff may not like the thought of larval therapy, but the treatment appears to have no adverse side-effects. Research into the therapy is continuing and further education for practitioners, in the form of study days and conferences, is available.

References

Baer, W.S. (1931) The treatment of chronic osteomyelitis with the maggot (larva of the blow fly). *Journal of Bone and Joint Surgery*; 13: 438–475.

Biosurgical Research Unit (1997) *Data Card*. Bridgend: Biosurgical Research Unit, Surgical Materials Testing Laboratory, Bridgend and District NHS Trust.

Bunkis, J. et al. (1985) Maggot therapy revisited. *Western Journal of Medicine*; 142: 554–556.

Jones, M. et al (1998) *A Case History Describing the Use of Sterile Larvae (Maggots) in a Malignant Wound*. World Wide Wounds: (www.smtl.co.uk/World-Wide-Wounds/Larvae-Case-Study-Malignant-Wounds-htm).

Larrey, Baron D. (1832) *Observations on Wounds and Their Complications by Erysipelas, Gangrene, and Tetanus, etc.* Translated from French by Rivinus, E.F. Philadelphia: Key, Miekle and Biddle.

McKeever, D.C. (1933) Maggots in the treatment of osteomyelitis: a simple inexpensive method. *Journal of Bone and Joint Surgery*; 15: 93.

Messer, F.C., McClellan, R.H. (1935) Surgical maggots: a study of their functions in wound healing. *Journal of Laboratory and Clinical Medicine*; 20: 1219.

Paré, A. (1579) *Les Oeuvres d'Ambroise Paré*. Translation from the Latin by Theodore Johnson, 1678. London: Clark.

Robinson, W. (1935) Stimulation of healing in non-healing wounds by allantoin occurring in maggot secretions and of wide biological distribution. *Journal of Bone and Joint Surgery*; 17: 267–271.

Robinson, W. (1940) Ammonium bicarbonate secreted by surgical maggots stimulates healing in purulent wounds. *American Journal of Surgery*; 47: 111–115.

Schmidt, R.J. et al (1993) Biocompatibility of wound management products. *Journal of Pharmacy and Pharmacology*; 45: 508–513.

Thomas, S. et al (1996) All you need to know about maggots. *Nursing Times*; 92: 46, 63–70.

United Kingdom Central Council for Nurses, Midwives and Health Visitors (1994) *Code of Professional Conduct*. London: UKCC.

Vistnes, L.M. et al (1981) Proteolytic activity of blowfly larvae secretions in experimental burns. *Surgery*; 90: 825–841.

Weil, G.C. et al (1931) The cultivation and sterilization of the fly larvae or maggot. *West Virginia Medical Journal*; 27: 458–461.

Zaccharias, J.F. (1904) Obituary. *Journal of the American Medical Association*; 43: 748.

13 Electrotherapies

Stephen Young
Kate Ballard

Key points

- ▶ The effectiveness of electrotherapies is dependent on a number of variables

- ▶ Ultrasound is the most commonly used electrotherapy and has been shown to be effective in stimulating wound healing

- ▶ Ultrasound can be used in the inflammatory, proliferative and remodelling stages of healing

- ▶ There is still a lack of hard evidence to support the claim that light is an effective tool for stimulating wound healing

- ▶ When used on cell cultures in laboratory conditions, light does produce biological effects; however, these have not been demonstrated clinically

Introduction

The aim of this chapter is to provide nurses with a reference source about electrotherapies. It will discuss what is known about the biological effects of the two main forms of electrotherapies in use, laser and ultrasound, on wound healing.

From the literature it is clear there is a large variation in the treatments' reported effectiveness. Some investigators have noted great improvements in healing rates, whereas others have reported disappointing results. From our review of the literature we think the variation depends upon a number of variables, the main ones being:

- ▶ type of electrotherapy used

- ▶ length of treatment

- ▶ output parameters of the electrotherapy; power, intensity, frequency and so on

- ► wound type

- ► stage of wound healing

- ► underlying chronic disease

- ► presence of infection

- ► concomitant therapy used

To use an electrotherapy effectively, a thorough understanding of the wound healing process is needed. It is apparent that some electrotherapies are only useful during certain stages of the repair process and not during others. This knowledge can save a lot of nursing/patient time and resources.

Wound repair

Immediately after injury a number of specialised chemical and cellular processes begin. Although wound healing is covered in detail in chapter 2, it is worth summarising the key processes here.

The major cells involved in wound healing are platelets, mast cells, polymorphonuclear leucocytes (PMNLs), macrophages, lymphocytes, endothelial cells and fibroblasts. These cells appear in the wound bed and take part in the healing process in a specific chronological sequence. This sequence is strictly controlled by the release of an array of chemicals called cytokines. Healing has shown to be adversely affected when either the cells, or the cytokines which control their actions, are inhibited. For a therapy to have a beneficial effect on healing its action will have to be directed at these targets.

Once the coagulation process, which involves platelets, thrombin, collagen and mast cells, is complete, a number of chemical mediators are liberated which kick-start the inflammatory phase of repair (Yurt, 1981).

Leucocytes are the first inflammatory cells to appear at the wound site. These are followed within a few hours by macrophages. The inflammatory phase normally lasts for several days then, as the wound moves into the proliferative phase, the inflammatory cells decrease and the number of fibroblasts and endothelial cells increase. The cytokines released by macrophages stimulate the fibroblasts to proliferate (Whal, 1981).

As the number of fibroblasts increases so does the level of collagen synthesis. Then as the cell population in the wound bed increases, so does the metabolic demand and endothelial cells increase, leading to a new capillary blood supply to the area developing.

This process of capillary development is known as angiogenesis. All of these processes are controlled by macrophage-derived cytokines (Banda et al, 1982; Polverini and Leibovich, 1984).

The final phase of repair is remodelling, where granulation tissue is replaced by scar tissue. Because scar tissue is an inferior substitute for normal skin, its development and possible replacement by more normal tissue is of considerable importance.

There are a number of electrotherapies currently being used which have been shown to have an effect on the healing process.

Ultrasound

Ultrasound is the most commonly used electrotherapy (Ter Haar et al, 1988). It has been shown to be effective in stimulating healing, but the degree of effectiveness is dependent on several parameters:

▶ power and intensity of the ultrasound

▶ length of treatment

▶ pulsing regime of the ultrasound

▶ phase of wound healing when the treatment is first applied

Ultrasound and the inflammatory phase of repair

The most dynamic phase of wound repair is the inflammatory phase, when numerous cell types such as platelets, mast cells, leucocytes and macrophages enter and leave the wound site.

Research has shown that therapeutic levels of ultrasound can affect the activity of these cells and hence the inflammatory phase of repair (Young and Dyson, 1990a). Williams et al (1974 and 1976) showed that ultrasound modified the permeability of the platelet membrane, leading to the release of seratonin.

The mast cell is a major source of histamine, a chemical central to modification of the wound environment immediately after injury. The mechanism by which the mast cell releases this chemical is called degranulation and is usually modulated by increases in intracellular calcium (Yurt, 1981).

A single treatment of ultrasound, if given shortly after injury, can stimulate mast cells to degranulate (Fyfe and Chahl, 1982; Hashish, 1986). There is evidence that ultrasound also alters the permeability of other cells, for example macrophages and fibroblasts (Young and Dyson, 1990a; Mummery, 1978; Mortimer and Dyson, 1988; Dinno et al, 1989).

The ability of ultrasound to alter the permeability of cell membranes to calcium ions is of considerable clinical importance, as changes in calcium levels can have a profound influence on cell metabolism.

Ultrasound has been shown to be effective in reducing post-operative oedema (El Hag et al, 1985; Fyfe and Chahl, 1985; Hustler et al, 1978). It accelerates the inflammatory phase, moving the wound into the proliferative phase of repair sooner.

Ultrasound and the proliferative phase of repair

The main cells involved in this phase are fibroblasts and endothelial cells. Fibroblasts move into the wound site and lay down new matrix, with the endothelial cells providing the new blood supply to the area. It has been shown that therapeutic ultrasound can increase fibroblast motility (Mummery, 1978).

Studies on wound biopsies after ultrasound therapy have shown that there are significantly more fibroblasts compared with untreated control wounds (Young and Dyson, 1990b).

Ultrasound also has an effect on the rate of angiogenesis. Hogan et al (1982) demonstrated that capillaries develop more rapidly in chronically ischaemic muscle when exposed to ultrasound.

Young and Dyson (1990c) showed that ultrasound increased the growth of capillaries into skin lesions.

Ultrasound has been found to increase collagen secretion from fibroblasts (Harvey et al, 1975). Hart (1993) showed that treatment with ultrasound can increase wound contraction and lead to a significant decrease in the final scar size. The most interesting point from this work was that the best effect was achieved at the lowest ultrasound intensity. When ultrasound is used at high intensities there is a risk of damage owing to excessive heating if used incorrectly (Young, 1996).

Clinical studies

Dyson et al (1976) found that they could stimulate the healing of varicose ulcers using therapeutic levels of ultrasound. Callam et al (1987) reported a 20% increase in the rate of healing when comparing varicose ulcers treated with ultrasound with untreated controls.

Other types of chronic wounds, such as pressure sores, have responded well to therapeutic ultrasound (Paul et al, 1960; McDiarmid et al, 1985).

McDiarmid reported that the ultrasound had an enhanced effect when used on infected wounds. A possible explanation is that the infection in some way primed the wound so the cells were more responsive to ultrasound therapy.

Not all trials have yielded positive results. Ter Riet et al (1995) reported no difference between groups when comparing ultrasound against placebo for the treatment of pressure sores. However, it is fair to say that most trials investigating the effect of therapeutic ultrasound on pressure sores have involved low numbers of subjects.

David Machin, chief medical statistician at the MRC Cancer Trials Office, commenting on Ter Reit's paper, said the trial contained too few subjects, as did other studies. He added: 'For such a common condition, what is needed is a large, pragmatic multicentre (multinational) double blind trial, comparing ultrasound treatment with placebo' (Machin, 1995).

Ultrasound and the remodelling phase of repair

Remodelling can last from months to years, depending upon the individual's ability to heal and the nature and site of their injury. During remodelling, tissue is converted from granulation to scar which is relatively acellular and avascular. Webster (1980) showed that scars of wounds treated with ultrasound during the remodelling phase were significantly stronger and more elastic compared to untreated controls.

There is little evidence to show that using ultrasound on mature scar tissue reduces its size or increases skin elasticity.

Summary

If used correctly, and at the correct time after injury, ultrasound can be an effective aid to wound healing. But if used incorrectly by an untrained operator, at best it will be ineffective, at worst extremely dangerous. Most of the problems can be avoided by using the lowest effective ultrasound intensity, that is below 1W per cm^2.

Low-level laser (light) therapy

There is a lack of objective clinical evidence to support the many claims that light is effective in stimulating healing. Doubts still exist as to the clinical efficacy of light and these are discussed in detail in two major publications (Basford, 1986; King, 1989).

There have been a number of laboratory studies, both *in vitro* and *in vivo*, demonstrating that biological effects can be induced in cells and tissues exposed to low levels of light.

The major cellular studies include work by Boulton and Marshall (1986), who demonstrated an increase in the proliferation of fibroblasts when exposed to light. Light has also been shown to stimulate collagen synthesis (Lam et al, 1986).

When macrophages are exposed to light of varying wavelengths and coherence they are stimulated to produce the wound mediators referred to as cytokines (Young et al, 1989).

The macrophage experiments showed that the effect was dependent on the wavelength of the light used, with light in the 660nm (red) part of the light spectrum being most effective. The effects of the light appeared to be independent of the coherence; that is, ordinary (non-coherent) light was as effective as laser (coherent) light.

Other work has shown that light energy appears to affect cellular activity by a non-thermal mechanism, possibly altering the cell membrane's permeability to calcium (Young et al, 1990d).

Most of the *in vivo* laboratory studies using animal acute wound models have shown that light can stimulate wounds to contract more rapidly (Dyson and Young, 1986). Other researchers have also demonstrated an acceleration in the healing process (Mester et al, 1975, 1985; Enwemeka et al, 1990; Abergel et al, 1987). However, some experiments have failed to show any cellular response to light (Hallman et al, 1988).

Animal model systems have proved useful in verifying that it is possible to produce desirable therapeutic effects on wounds, but it has proved more difficult to demonstrate this effect in humans. The literature is contradictory, with some investigators reporting positive effects, others no effect at all (Basford, 1986; King, 1989).

The problem to date with most human clinical trials has been the lack of controls in the patient population and small sample sizes. Most reports are anecdotal and should be classed as case studies, not clinical trials.

Many studies do not state clearly what their treatment parameters were, for example, laser power, pulse frequency, wavelength, treatment time period, frequency of treatments and so on. This means it is impossible to replicate another investigator's work to achieve the positive result. The variations between individual investigator's studies also mean it is impossible to combine the results to derive optimum treatment regimes. Some anecdotal evidence does indicate that light can produce biological effects in human wounds (Baxter et al, 1991; Mester and Mester, 1989; Sugrue et al, 1990; Fenyo, 1984; Karu, 1985).

Summary

Unlike ultrasound, evidence for the effectiveness of light/laser therapy is sparse. Funding has not been forthcoming to put this therapy to the test in large, multi-centre, randomised controlled clinical trials. The weight of clinical evidence is largely anecdotal.

This is not to say that light therapy does not work. There is a large body of evidence showing that light does produce biological effects when used on cell cultures in strictly controlled laboratory conditions. The major problem has been translating this into effective use in the clinical environment.

References

Abergel, R.P. et al (1987) Biostimulation of wound healing by lasers: experimental approaches in animal models and fibroblast cultures. *Journal of Dermatological Surgery Oncology*; 13: 127–133.

Banda, M.J. et al (1982) Isolation of a nonmitogenic angiogenesis factor from wound fluid. *Proceedings of the National Academy of Science*. USA. 79: 7773–7777.

Basford, J.K. (1986). Low-energy treatment of pain and wounds: hype, hope or hokum? *Mayo Clinic Proceedings*; 61: 671–675.

Baxter, G.D. et al (1991) Low level laser therapy: current clinical practice in Northern Ireland. *Physiotherapy*; 77: 171–178.

Boulton, M., Marshall, J. (1986) He-Ne laser stimulation of human fibroblast proliferation and attachment *in vitro*. *Lasers in Life Sciences*; 1: 125–134.

Callam, M.J. et al (1987) A controlled trial of weekly ultrasound therapy in chronic leg ulceration. *Lancet*; 25: 204–-206.

Dinno, M.A. et al (1989) The significance of membrane changes in the safe and effective use of therapeutic and diagnostic. *Physics in Medicine and Biology*; 34: 1543–1552.

Dyson, M. et al (1976) Stimulation of healing varicose ulcers by ultrasound. *Ultrasonics*; 14: 232–236.

Dyson, M., Young, S.R. (1986) The effect of laser therapy on wound contraction and cellularity. *Lasers in Medical Science*; 1: 125–130.

Dyson, M. et al (1988) Comparison of the effects of moist and dry conditions on dermal repair. *Journal of Investigative Dermatology*; 91: 434–439.

El Hag, M. et al (1985) The anti-inflammatory effects of dexamethasone and therapeutic ultrasound in oral surgery. *British Journal of Oral Maxillofacial Surgery*; 23: 17–23.

Enwemeka, C.S. et al (1990) Correlative ultrastructural and biomedical changes induced in regenerating tendons exposed to laser photostimulation. *Lasers Surgery Medicine*; 2: Supplement, 12.

Fenyo, M. (1984) Theoretical and experimental basis of biostimulation by laser irradiation. *Optics and Laser Technology*; ,209–215.

Fyfe, M.C., Chahl, L.A. (1982) Mast cell degranulation: a possible mechanism of action of therapeutic ultrasound. *Ultrasound in Medicine and Biology*; 8: (Supplement 1), 62.

Fyfe, M.C., Chahl, L.A. (1985) The effect of single or repeated applications of 'therapeutic' ultrasound on plasma extravasation during silver induced inflammation of the rat hindpaw ankle joint *in vivo*. *Ultrasound in Medicine and Biology*; 11: 273–283.

Ter Haar, G. et al (1988) Ultrasound in physiotherapy in the United Kingdom; results of a questionnaire. *Physiotherapy Practice*; 4: 69–72.

Hallman, H.O. et al (1988) Does low energy He-Ne laser irradiation alter *in vitro* replication of human fibroblasts? *Lasers Surgery Medicine;* 8: 125–129.

Harvey, W. et al (1975) The stimulation of proteinsynthesis in human fibroblasts by therapeutic ultrasound. *Rheumatology and Rehabilitation;* 14: 237.

Hashish, I. (1986) *The Effects of Ultrasound Therapy on Postoperative Inflammation* (PhD thesis). London: University of London.

Hogan, R.D.B. et al (1982) The effect of ultrasound on the microvascular hemodynamics in skeletal muscle: effects during ischaemia. *Microvascular Research;* 23: 70–379.

Karu, T.I. (1985) Biological action of low-intensity visible monochromatic light and some of its medical applications. *International Congress on Lasers in Medicine and Surgery;* June 26–28, 25–29.

King, P.R. (1989) Low level laser therapy: a review. *Lasers in Medical Science;* 4: 141–150.

Lam, T. et al (1986) Low energy lasers selectively enhance collagen synthesis. *Lasers Life Sciences;* 1: 61–77.

McDiarmid, T. et al (1985) Ultrasound and the treatment of pressure sores. *Physiotherapy;* 71: 66–70.

Machin, D. (1995) Ultrasound treatment for pressure ulcers (letter; comment); 311: 6996, 57. *Lasers Life Sciences;* 1, 61–77.

Mester, E. et al (1975) The effect of laser irradiation on the regeneration of muscle fibres. *Zeitschrift Experimentelle Chirurgie;* 8: 258–262.

Mester, E. et al (1985) The biomedical effects of laser application. *Lasers Surgery Medicine;* 5: 31–39.

Mester, A.F., Mester, A. (1989) Wound healing. *Laser Therapy;* 1: 7-15.

Metchnikof, E. (1891) *Lectures on the Comparative Pathology of Inflammation.* New York: Dover.

Mortimer, A.J., Dyson, M. (1988) The effect of therapeutic ultrasound on calcium uptake in fibroblasts. *Ultrasound in Medicine and Biology;* 14: 499–506.

Mummery, C.L. (1978) *The Effect of Ultrasound on Fibroblasts in Vitro.* (PhD thesis). London: University of London.

Paul. B.J. et al (1960) Use of ultrasound in the treatment of pressure sores in patients with spinal cord injuries. *Archives of Physical Medicine in Rehabilitation;* 41: 438–440.

Polverini, P.J., Leibovich, J.S. (1984) Induction of neovascularisation *in vivo* by tumor associated macrophages. *Laboratory Investigations;* 51: 35–642.

Ross, R., Benditt, E.P. (1961) Wound healing and collagen formation: 1. Sequential changes in components of guinea pig skin wounds observed in the electron microscope. *Journal of Biophysics Biochemistry and Cytology;* 11: 677–700.

Sugrue, M.E. et al (1990). The use of infra-red laser therapy in the treatment of venous ulceration. *Annals of Vascular Surgery;* 4: 2, 179–181.

Ter Riet, G. et al (1995) Randomised clinical trial of ultrasound treatment for pressure sores. *British Medical Journal;* 310: 1040–1041.

Webster, D.F. (1980) *The Effect of Ultrasound on Wound Healing*. (PhD thesis). London: University of London.

Whal, S.M. (1981) The role of mononuclear cells in the wound repair process. In: Dineen, P., Hildick-Smith, G. (eds) *The Surgical Wound*. Philadelphia: Lea and Ferbiger.

Williams, A.R. (1974) The release of seratonin from platelets by acoustic streaming. *Journal of the Acoustical Society of America*; 56: 1640.

Williams, A.R. et al (1976) Ultrasonic exposure modifies platelet morphology and function in vitro. *Ultrasound in Medicine and Biology*; 2: 311–317.

Young, S.R. et al (1989) Macrophage responsiveness to laser therapy. *Lasers in Surgery and Medicine*; 9, 497–505.

Young, S.R., Dyson, M. (1990a) Macrophage responsiveness to therapeutic ultrasound. *Ultrasound in Medicine and Biology*; 16: 09–816.

Young, S.R., Dyson, M. (1990b) The effect of therapeutic ultrasound on the healing of full-thickness excised skin lesions. *Ultrasonics*; 28: 175–180.

Young, S.R., Dyson, M. (1990c) The effect of therapeutic ultrasound on angiogenesis. *Ultrasound in Medicine and Biology*; 16: 261–269.

Young, S.R. et al (1990d) The effect of light on calcium uptake in macrophages. *Laser Therapy*; 2: 2, 53–57.

Yurt, R.W. (1981) Role of the mast cell in trauma. In: Dineen, P., Hildick-Smith, G. (eds) *The Surgical Wound*; Philadelphia: Lea and Ferbiger.

14 Hyperbaric therapy

Sally Simmons

Key points

▶ Hyperbaric oxygen therapy (HBOT) has been in use since the 1950s

▶ HBOT is the intermittent breathing of 100% oxygen at greater than atmospheric pressure

▶ The Undersea and Hyperbaric Medical Society has established accepted indications for use

▶ HBOT can be useful in treating some chronic wounds

Introduction

Clinical hyperbaric oxygen therapy (HBOT) has been used since about 1955, beginning with the work of Churchill-Davidson (1955) and Boerema et al (1956), although the use of compressed air in chambers was described as early as 1879 by Fontaine.

The Undersea and Hyperbaric Medical Society (UHMS) established the Committee on HBOT in 1976 to explore the evolving clinical applications of this treatment. They published their first report the following year (Camporesi, 1977) which showed that wounds were among these applications, and they now constitute the majority of hyperbaric medicine practice, particularly in the USA (Hunt, 1996).

Definition

HBOT is the intermittent breathing of 100% oxygen at greater than atmospheric pressure. Essentially, it is a way of administrating a higher dose of oxygen than is possible at normal atmospheric pressure. Oxygen is therefore used as a drug and has a defined therapeutic dose range and toxicity effects (Hammarlund, 1995).

Indications for use

The following are the UHMS accepted indications for hyperbaric medicine (UHMS, 1996):

▶ carbon monoxide poisoning and smoke inhalation

▶ air or gas embolism

▶ crush injury, compartment syndrome and other acute traumatic ischaemias

▶ clostridial myonecrosis (gas gangrene)

▶ decompression illness

▶ enhancement of healing in selected problem wounds

▶ exceptional blood loss anaemia

▶ necrotising soft tissue infections

▶ osteomyelitis (refractory)

▶ radiation tissue damage (osteoradionecrosis)

▶ skin grafts and flaps (compromised)

▶ thermal burns

▶ adjunctive hyperbaric oxygen in intracranial abscess

Case history

Peter Crookbain, a 70-year-old semi-retired engineer, had already undergone five operations on his left ankle, starting with an osteotomy in 1995. An ankle replacement was carried out in October 1997, but he subsequently fractured his medial malleolus following a fall. He then developed an infection and severe septicaemia. The ankle prosthesis was removed in December after which a bone graft was applied with external fixation. When the fixation was removed, a deep wound was left which contained a sinus and some foul-smelling exudate (Plate 1).

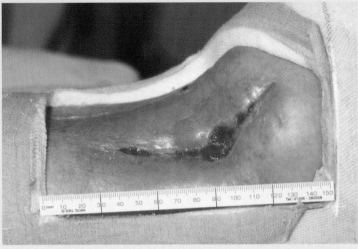

Plate 1

Although a window had been cut into the synthetic plaster to facilitate wound access, it was extremely difficult to dress adequately. A swab was taken on the first visit and the wound was mapped. *Pseudomonas aeruginosa* was grown, so the wound was treated for two days with silver sulphadiazine.

The consultant's referral letter stated that larval therapy had been used and maggots should still be present in the wound. It appeared that at least half of these had survived the initial pressurisation. (The use of maggots in conjunction with HBOT and wound healing requires further research.) However, the wound was exuding heavily, and it was clear the maggots were unable to cope with this amount of fluid production. They were removed and a new plaster applied so the wound was more accessible.

Dressings were changed daily prior to HBOT. Calcium alginate dressings covered with gauze swabs and a light bandage were effective combined with antibiotics and HBOT.

The patient received 30 daily treatments of HBOT at 2.4 bar for a total of approximately one hour 40 minutes per treatment. Plate 2 depicts the healing wound.

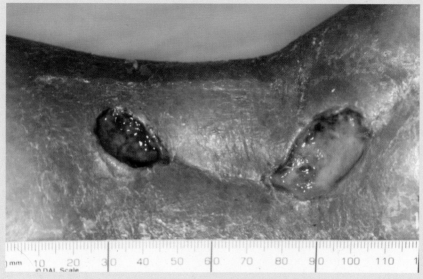

Plate 2

Hyperbaric oxygen therapy

Patients are treated either in steel chambers, such as the multiplace (Plate 3), or steel and acrylic chambers, as in the monoplace (Plate 4). Multiplace chambers can treat more than one patient at a time.

Patients breathe 100% oxygen via a hood system (Plate 5). The oxygen dose depends on the pressure; so at 2.4 bar the patient breathes 2.4 times the amount of oxygen breathed at normal atmospheric pressure (Hammarlund, 1995).

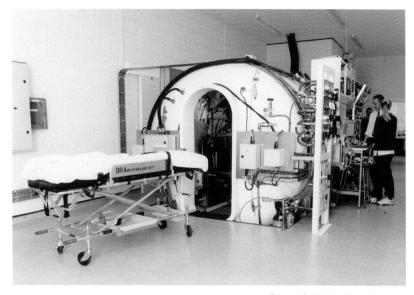

Plate 3 Multiplace chamber

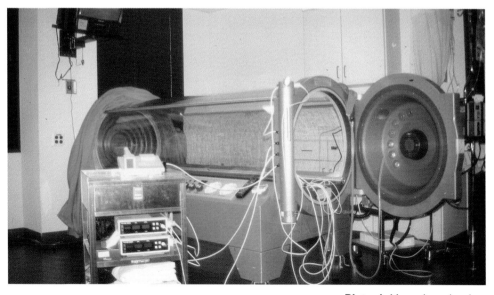

Plate 4 Monoplace chamber

Plate 5 HBOT hood system

Pharmacology of hyperbaric oxygen

Hyperbaric oxygen is a drug, so it has a therapeutic index, where a higher dose is toxic (Clarke, 1982) and a lower dose ineffective (Hammarlund, 1995). Arterial blood contains approximately 20ml oxygen per 100ml of blood, but the body requires approximately 6ml of oxygen per 100ml of blood for metabolic processes, normally provided by the haemoglobin. At a pressure of 3 bar, for example, not only is arterial oxygen 25.3ml per 100ml of blood, but 5.6ml of oxygen per 100ml of blood are dissolved in the plasma. In a patient with a diminished ability to carry oxygen in the haemoglobin, this has clear implications for improving tissue oxygenation.

One effect of high-dose oxygen on the vasculature is vasoconstriction and reduced blood flow (Kindwall, 1995). Normally, one would expect this to cause hypoxia, but the greatly increased oxygen content of the plasma maintains tissue oxygen delivery. In the context of wound healing, HBOT reduces tissue oedema, directly improving tissue oxygenation.

Ischaemia-reperfusion injury

Prolonged periods of ischaemia followed by reperfusion can lead to complete microcirculatory failure and cell death. This condition is known as ischaemia-reperfusion injury and is linked to oxygen-free radical production during the reperfusion phase (Zamboni, 1995).

Ischaemia-reperfusion injury can occur when patients suffer high-energy trauma, compartment syndromes, amputated body parts or compromised flaps. Tissue ischaemia occurs and, despite successful efforts to restore perfusion, the microcirculation subsequently collapses and tissue necrosis ensues.

HBOT in ischaemia-reperfusion injury

Oxygen-free radical production in ischaemia-reperfusion (I-R) injury has been explored by Feller et al (1989). Oxygen-free radicals are extremely toxic, unstable molecules which cause cell death by lipid peroxidation and propagation of more free radicals. There is also evidence of increased leucocyte-endothelial adherence owing in part to free radical production (Zamboni, 1989). This can lead to progressive arteriolar vasoconstriction and the deleterious cascade of events following reperfusion.

The use of HBOT in the adjunctive treatment of I-R injury has been controversial because it adds extra oxygen to the system and increases free radical production (Behnke, 1988). However, HBOT has been shown to be beneficial rather than detrimental, inhibiting the production of free radicals systemically (Zamboni et al, 1989; Zamboni et al, 1993). Although the mechanism for this is not yet fully understood, one possibility is that HBOT has a direct effect on leucocyte adherence.

Zamboni advises early treatment of I-R injury using HBOT adjunctively, and provides anecdotal evidence of satisfactory outcomes in patients with up to 14 hours' ischaemia using surgery followed immediately by HBOT (Kindwall, 1995). A multi-centre prospective randomised trial is needed to support these findings.

Wound healing

Wound healing is orchestrated by a complex interaction of biochemical and physiological mechanisms (Hunt, 1979). These mechanisms initiate, regulate and discontinue the biological events of the healing process. Rational treatment strategies must take these mechanisms into account if they are to be of optimal use.

It is important to remember there is no place for HBOT in normally healing, uncomplicated wounds and that HBOT is an adjunct to the conventional treatment of problem wounds.

The role of oxygen in wound healing

At different phases of the wound healing process, both hypoxia and normal amounts of oxygen are required. The area between the wound edges, which contain clotted blood and tissue debris, is termed the wound space (Knighton, 1995).

This space is small in sutured wounds but larger in unsutured wounds and burns. It is hypoxic (0–15mmHg) due to the lack of a microcirculation and increased cellular activity at the wound edge, which consumes large amounts of oxygen (Silver, 1966).

Hypoxia is required for macrophages to produce angiogenic factors and mitogens which stimulate fibroblast replication (Knighton et al, 1984). If the oxygen gradient across the wound from space to edge is diminished because the wound edge is poorly perfused and hypoxic, healing will be impaired (La Van and Hunt, 1990).

This is because fibroblast proliferation and the ability to provide normal collagen is diminished at oxygen tensions of less than 30mmHg (Knighton, 1995). Tissue oxygen tensions greater than 30mmHg are necessary for the hydroxylation of lysine and proline, an essential biochemical reaction in the formation of collagen by fibroblasts. The rate of collagen formation increases as the tissue oxygen tension is increased from 30mmHg to about 100mmHg (Heimbach, 1997).

Oxygen and infection

Phagocytic polymorphonucleoleucocytes (PMN) are the body's primary cellular defence mechanism. They phagocytose but are unable to kill bacteria in hypoxic tissue (Mandell, 1974). The efficiency of the PMNs will increase up to a tissue pO_2 of 150mmHg (Mader et al, 1980). This is important in treating *Clostridium perfringens*, which is the main clostridium organism implicated in gas gangrene.

Demello et al (1970) concluded that increased oxygen tensions may only have a small direct role in the destruction of *Clostridium perfringens*. The more important effect was the indirect influence on PMNs.

HBOT also inhibits the production of clostridial alpha-toxin, which destroys cell membranes and increases capillary permeability (Heimbach, 1991).

Hyperbaric oxygen is bacteriostatic to anaerobic and microaerophilic organisms and, as it produces vasoconstriction with maintenance of oxygenation, oedema is reduced (Zamboni 1993). HBOT is effective in conjunction with certain antimicrobials (Box 1). It is thought that HBOT raises the PO_2 of hypoxic tissue to normal levels, which normalises antimicrobial activity (Jonsson et al, 1990; Park et al, 1995).

▶ Elevation of the PO_2 of ischaemic tissue to levels required for optimal activity of certain antimicrobial agents. Examples are aminoglycosides, certain sulphonamides, fluroquinolone, trimethoprim and vancomycin

▶ Inhibition of bacterial biosynthetic reactions. Examples are the potentiation of the activity of sulphonamides and the prolongation of the post-antibiotic effect of aminoglycosides in pseudomonas infections

▶ Lowering of the oxidation reduction potential in bacteria. Examples are increased production of reactive intermediates (nitrofurantoin) and decreased activation of antimicrobial agents dependent on low redox potential (metronidazole)

Box 1 Mechanism by which HBOT influences the activity of antimicrobial agents (Kindwall, 1995)

Problem wounds

The Wagner Classification (Table 1) categorises diabetic foot lesions by depth of tissue involvement, presence and extent of infection and presence of gangrene. Adjunctive HBOT is usually reserved for grade 3 and 4 lesions. Once a healthy granulation bed has appeared HBOT can be discontinued. This usually occurs after about 20–30 treatments (Matos and Nunez, 1995; Faglia, 1996).

The main objective in treating these lesions is to minimise tissue loss and promote granulation and epithelial growth. This ultimately results in a healed, functioning foot.

Grade 0	The skin is intact. There is no open lesion. There may be bony deformities, Charcot joint changes and partial amputations such as toe or transmetatarsal
Grade 1	There is a superficial ulcer without penetration to deep layers
Grade 2	The ulcer is deeper and reaches tendon, bone or joint capsule
Grade 3	Deeper tissues are involved and there is osteomyelitis, plantar space abscess or tendonitis usually with extension along the midfoot compartments of tendon sheaths. Operative debridement is mandatory
Grade 4	There is gangrene of some portion of the toe, toes, and/or forefoot. The gangrene may be wet or dry, infected or non-infected, but in general surgical ablation of a portion of the toe or foot is indicated
Grade 5	Gangrene involves the whole foot or enough of the foot that no local procedures are possible and amputation must be carried out, at least at the below knee level

Table 1 Wagner diabetic foot classification (Wagner, 1981)

Treating venous ulceration

HBOT can be used to treat chronic venous ulceration but other, cheaper, proven methods such as external compression and local wound management should be the mainstay of treatment.

Irradiated wounds, such as those that occur in osteoradionecrosis, are also problematic because they are hypocellular, hypoxic and hypovascular (Marx, 1983). Radiotherapy does not limit itself to the cancerous lesion but can damage the healthy surrounding skin (Heimbach, 1985). In time this becomes progressively more fibrous and therefore more hypoxic owing to the loss of blood vessels. Wound breakdown is common and this can cause considerable distress to the patient.

HBOT's effect on irradiated wounds is to promote capillary angiogenesis and fibroplasia (Marx et al, 1990). Histologic changes in irradiated tissue can be seen after eight HBOT treatments. These show macrophage activity, fibroblastic collagen production and endothelial proliferation (Marx and Johnson, 1988).

Other conditions treated with agreed protocols are osteomyelitis (Britt et al, 1995), hypoxic skin grafts and flaps (Nemiroff, 1995) and certain necrotising skin infections, such as Fournier's gangrene, which involve bacterial synergism (Bakker and Kox, 1988).

Wound assessment

Measuring tissue oxygen tension transcutaneously is routine in the assessment of wounds before HBOT. The use of transcutaneous oxygen ($TcPO_2$) monitoring devices has proved cost-effective and there is sufficient published clinical evidence to support its use (Sheffield and Workman, 1983).

TcPO$_2$ measurement is important for several reasons:

▶ it is a tool used in medical decision making to aid vascular assessment, to select suitable candidates for HBOT and to determine when treatment is complete

▶ it provides direct, continuous quantitative assessment of oxygen availability

▶ direct relationships have been proved between wound oxygen tension, resistance to infection and wound healing (Matos and Nunez, 1995)

Conclusion

HBOT is not a new, untried treatment, but there is a need for further, well-controlled, prospective studies in the field of problem wound healing so that the full effectiveness of HBOT can be defined.

The recognised applications have been scientifically researched worldwide over the past 50 years, and there is a considerable amount of research being undertaken at present to discover other disease applications.

Its use in problem wound healing constitutes the vast majority of HBOT undertaken in the USA. In this country, as hyperbaric therapy becomes increasingly available and less expensive, instead of being relegated to 'a treatment looking for a disease' (Hunt, 1996), it may take its rightful place in the forefront of modern medical and nursing practice.

References

Bakker, D., Kox, C. (1988) Classification and therapy of necrotizing soft tissue infections: the role of surgery, antibiotics and hyperbaric oxygen. *Current Problems in General Surgery*; 5: 4, 489–500.

Bartlett, R.L. et al (1998) Rabbit model of the use of fasciotomy and hyperbaric oxygen therapy in the treatment of compartment syndrome. *Proceedings of the Undersea and Hyperbaric Medical Society Annual Scientific Conference*; 5: 28.

Behnke, P.J. (1988) Jessica in the well: ischaemia-reperfusion injury. *Journal of American Medical Association*; 259: 9, 1326.

Boerema, I. et al (1956) High atmospheric pressure as an aid to cardiac surgery. *Archives of Surgery of the Netherlands*; 8:2,193-211.

Britt, M. et al (1995) The use of hyperbaric oxygen in the treatment of osteomyelitis. In: Kindwall, E.P. (ed.) *Hyperbaric Medicine Practice*. Arizona: Best Publishing Company.

Camporesi, E.M. (1977) Undersea and Hyperbaric Medicine Society. *Hyperbaric Oxygen Therapy: A Committee Report*. Bethesda: UHMS.

Camporesi, E.M. (1996) Undersea and Hyperbaric Medicine Society. *Hyperbaric Oxygen Therapy: A Committee Report*. Kensington: UHMS.

Churchill-Davidson, I. et al (1955) High pressure oxygen and radiotherapy. *Lancet*; 1: 6874, 1091–1095.

Clarke, J.M. (1982) Oxygen toxicity. In: Bennett, P.B., Elliott, D.H. (eds) *The Physiology and Medicine of Diving* (3rd edition). London: Baillière Tindall.

Demello, F.J. et al (1970) The effect of hyperbaric oxygen on the germination and toxin production of *Clostridium perfringens* spores. In: Wada, J., Iwa, J.T. (eds) *Proceedings of the Fourth International Congress on Hyperbaric Medicine*. Baltimore: Williams and Wilkins.

Faglia, P. (1996) Adjunctive systemic hyperbaric oxygen therapy in treatment of severe prevalently ischaemic diabetic foot ulcer. *Diabetes Care*; 19: 12, 1338–1343.

Feller, A.M. et al (1989) Experimental evaluation of oxygen free radical scavengers in the prevention of reperfusion injury to skeletal muscle. *Annals of Plastic Surgery*; 22: 4, 321.

Fontaine, J.A. (1879) Emploi chirugicale de l'aire comprime. *Un Medic*; 28, 448.

Hammarlund, C. (1995) The physiologic effects of hyperbaric oxygen, In: Kindwall, E.P. (ed.) *Hyperbaric Medicine Practice*. Arizona: Best Publishing Company.

Heimbach, R.D. (1985) Radiation effects on tissue. In: Davis, J.C., Hunt, T.K. (eds) *Problem Wounds: The Role of Oxygen*. New York: Elsevier.

Heimbach, R.D. (1991) Clostridial myonecrosis. In: Camporesi, E.M., Barker, A.C. (eds) *Hyperbaric Oxygen Therapy: A Critical Review*. Bethesda: Undersea and Hyperbaric Medical Society.

Heimbach, R.D. (1997) Biochemistry of Wound Healing. In: *Hyperbaric Medicine Team Training*. San Antonio: J.C. Davis Wound Care Center.

Hunt, T.K. (1979) Disorders of repair and their management. In: Hunt, T.K., Dunphy, J.E. (eds) *Fundamentals of Wound Management*. New York: Appleton-Century-Crofts.

Hunt, T.K. (1996) In: Undersea and Hyperbaric Medicine Society *Hyperbaric Oxygen Therapy: A Committee Report*. Kensington: UHMS.

Jonsson, K. et al (1990) Oxygen as an isolated variable influences resistance to infection. *Annals of Surgery*; 125: 5, 607–609.

Kindwall, E.P. (1995) The use of drugs under pressure. In: Kindwall, E.P. (ed.) *Hyperbaric Medicine Practice*. Arizona: Best Publishing Company.

Knighton, D.R. (1995) Mechanisms of wound healing. In: Kindwall, E.P. (ed.) *Hyperbaric Medicine Practice*. Arizona: Best Publishing Company.

Knighton, D.R. et al (1984) Regulation of repair: hypoxic control of macrophage mediated angiogenesis. In: Hunt, T.K., et al (eds). *Soft and Hard Tissue Repair*. New York: Praeser.

La Van, F.B., Hunt, T.K. (1990) Oxygen and wound healing. *Clinical Plastic Surgery*; 17: 3, 472.

Mader, J.T. et al (1980) A mechanism for the amelioration by hyperbaric oxygen therapy of experimental staphylococcal osteomyelitis in rabbits. *Journal of Infectious Diseases*; 142: 6, 915–922.

Mandell,G.L. (1974) Bactericidal activity of aerobic and anaerobic polymorphonuclear neutrophils. *Infection and Immunity*; 9: 2, 337–341.

Marx, R.E. (1983) A new concept in the treatment of osteoradionecrosis. *Journal of Oral and Maxillofacial Surgeons*; 41: 6, 351–357.

Marx, R.E., Johnson, R.P. (1988). Problem wounds in oral and maxillofacial surgery: The role of hyperbaric oxygen. In: Davis, J.C., Hunt, T.K. (eds) *Problem Wounds: The Role of Oxygen*. New York: Elsevier.

Marx, R.E. et al (1990) Relationship of oxygen dose to angiogenesis induction in irradiated tissue. *American Journal of Surgery;* 160: 5, 519–524.

Matos, L., Nunez, A. (1995) Enhancement of healing in selected problem wounds. In: Kindwall, E.P. (ed.) *Hyperbaric Medicine Practice.* Arizona: Best Publishing Company.

Nemiroff, P. (1995) Hyperbaric oxygen in skin grafts and flaps. In: Kindwall, E.P. (ed.) *Hyperbaric Medicine Practice.* Arizona: Best Publishing Company.

Park, M.K. et al (1995) Effects of hyperbaric oxygen on infectious diseases: basic mechanisms. In: Kindwall, E.P. (ed.) *Hyperbaric Medicine Practice.* Arizona: Best Publishing Company.

Sheffield, P.J., Workman, W.T. (1983) Transcutaneous tissue oxygen monitoring in patients undergoing hyperbaric oxygen therapy. In: Huch, R., Huch, A. (eds) *Continuous Blood Gas Monitoring.* New York: Marcel Dekker.

Silver, I.A. (1966) The measurement of oxygen tension in healing tissue. *International Anaesiology Clinics;* 4: 1, 124–135.

Strauss, M. (1995) Crush injury and other acute traumatic peripheral ischaemias. In: Kindwall, E.P. (ed.) *Hyperbaric Medicine Practice.* Arizona: Best Publishing Company.

Wagner, F.W. (1981) The dysvascular foot: a system for diagnosis and treatment. *Foot and Ankle;* 2: 5, 64–122.

Zamboni, W.A. et al (1989) The effect of acute hyperbaric oxygen therapy on axial pattern skin flap survival when administered during and after total ischaemia. *Journal of Reconstructive Microsurgery;* 5: 4, 343.

Zamboni, W.A. et al (1993) Morphologic analysis of the microcirculation during reperfusion of ischaemic skeletal muscle and the effect of hyperbaric oxygen. *Plastic and Reconstructive Surgery;* 91: 6, 1110–1123.

Zamboni, W.A. (1995) The microcirculation and ischaemia-reperfusion injury: basic mechanisms of hyperbaric oxygen therapy. In: Kindwall, E.P. (ed.) *Hyperbaric Medicine Practice.* Arizona: Best Publishing Company.

15 Growth factors

Jeff Hart

Key points

▶ Growth factors elicit a complex array of responses in receptive cells

▶ They are thought to be involved in stimulating and controlling all aspects of wound healing

▶ Growth factor therapy in itself does not address the underlying pathophysiologies that give rise to chronic wounds

▶ Pharmacologic intervention in the form of growth factor therapy, used in the context of a holistic approach to treatment, will prove to be an important weapon in the war on chronic wounds

Introduction

The term 'growth factors' refers to an assortment of small, naturally occurring proteins (peptides) which are thought to direct a variety of biological processes including embryological development, tumour growth and wound repair. When the term was first coined over 20 years ago it referred to factors that, when introduced to cultured cells, resulted in cell proliferation (that is, cell growth). More recently, the term has been used as an all-encompassing expression to describe a diverse group of protein-based multifunctional cell signalling molecules that can elicit a complex array of responses in receptive cells.

Following injury, growth factors are thought to be centrally involved in stimulating and controlling all aspects of the wound healing process. These include inflammatory cell recruitment, re-epithelialisation, fibroplasia, angiogenesis and the maturation of new dermal tissue to form a scar (Table 1).

Growth factor names can be both confusing and misleading. Some growth factors are named after the natural sources from which they were first isolated (for example, platelet-derived growth factor – PDGF), whereas most derive from biological responses observed during initial experimental investigations (for example, fibroblast growth factor – FGF – which was first observed to promote fibroblast proliferation *in vitro* and is now known primarily as a potent angiogenic agent).

The majority of growth factors have retained their original name. Some, however, have been renamed (for example, epidermal growth factor (EGF) originally known as urogastrone). Others, particularly those that have only recently been discovered, have more than one name, such as keratinocyte growth factor (KGF), also known as fibroblast growth factor-7 (FGF-7). A given growth factor may have a variety of forms, often termed isotypes. For example, PDGF, which is not one but two polypeptides joined together, can exist in three forms, PDGF-AA, AB and BB; depending on how the two possible PDGF polypeptide chains, PDGF-A and PDGF-B, are combined.

Until recently, growth factors were only available in very small amounts from their natural sources. New developments in the biotechnology industry, however, have resulted in large-scale growth factor production. Growth factors produced in this way are called recombinant growth factors (for example, recombinant human basic fibroblast growth factor – rhbFGF).

Basics

A variety of cells produce very small amounts of an assortment of growth factors under normal physiological conditions. This production can be increased in response to chemical and physical challenges, such as occur during the process of wounding. Once synthesised and released, most growth factors remain viable for only short periods of time unless they are bound to specific binding proteins or stabilised on matrix components.

In order for a growth factor to interact and stimulate activity in a cell, the recipient cell must possess specific growth factor receptors on its cell membrane. Growth factors signalling is described in terms of site of production, cellular recipient and the route between the two. Autocrine signalling indicates that a given cell releases a growth factor that activates its own receptors; whereas paracrine signalling indicates that growth factors produced by one cell are received and elicit a response in neighbouring cells.

Endocrine (hormonal) signalling involves relatively long-distance transport of growth factors from producer cells to effector cells, via the bloodstream. The fourth and least widely recognised form, juxtacrine signalling, involves direct cell-to-cell contact between cells expressing membrane-anchored growth factors and cells expressing specific growth factor receptors (Bosenberg and Massague, 1993).

Binding of a growth factor to its receptor activates the receptor and subsequently initiates a sequence of intracellular events. This transmits the growth factor signal to various sites within the cell, including the nucleus.

Rationale for growth factor therapy

The rationale for using growth factors to counteract chronic or delayed repair is based on a large body of experimental evidence that suggests that these factors:

▶ are both produced by, and can stimulate, cells involved in wound repair (Hart et al, 1990; Werner et al, 1992; Reuterdahl et al, 1993)

▶ have a central role in normal repair, as demonstrated by growth factor neutralisation studies (Broadley et al, 1989)

▶ can promote normal repair (Mustoe et al, 1987; Schultz et al, 1987; McGee et al, 1988)

▶ correct wound healing impairments in a wide variety of animal models (Mustoe et al, 1989; Pierce et al, 1989; Greenhalgh et al, 1990)

The main assumption for using growth factor treatments to promote repair is that chronic wounds are in a state of healing arrest and require stimulation to proceed with the repair process. Several researchers have reported that this healing arrest is paralleled by deficiencies in growth factor activity (Schmidt et al, 1993; Cooper et al, 1994; Pierce et al, 1995). These observations provide a biological basis for growth factor supplementation of chronic wounds.

Clinical studies

To date, clinical investigations on wound repair have concentrated on a limited range of growth factors including:

▶ basic fibroblast growth factor (bFGF)

▶ platelet-derived growth factor-BB (PDGF-BB)

▶ transforming growth factor-β2 (TGF-β2)

▶ epidermal growth factor (EGF)

▶ interleukin-1β (IL-1β)

▶ the degranulated platelet preparation – platelet-derived wound healing formula (PDWHF)

Growth factor treatment has been evaluated as a therapeutic approach with which to stimulate repair in a variety of tissues, including the repair of corneal damage (Dellaert et al, 1997), periodontal disease (Howell et al, 1997) and oral ulceration (Girdler et al, 1995). This review is, however, restricted to published studies involving growth factor treatment of cutaneous wounds (Table 2).

Fibroblast growth factors (FGFs)

FGFs are a group of similar polypeptides of which bFGF (also known as FGF-2, acidic fibroblast growth factor), aFGF (also known as FGF-1) and keratinocyte growth factor or KG, (also known as FGF-7) have been most extensively studied.

Basic FGF, which is released following cell damage, is a very potent angiogenic agent (Pierce eet al, 1992) also known for its ability to promote the proliferation of fibroblasts and epithelial cells (Maciag et al, 1994). The importance of bFGF in wound repair has been suggested by various pre-clinical studies. Reduced FGF expression has been observed in several animal models of delayed healing (Shukla et al, 1998) and the introduction of bFGF neutralising antibodies has been shown to have a significant delaying effect on acute wound repair (Mondain et al, 1995).

The ability of bFGF to promote normal repair and correct delayed repair has been demonstrated in animal studies (Fina et al, 1991; Greenhalgh et al, 1990; Tanaka et al, 1996).

Clinical investigations are restricted to the study of bFGF and, while initial results suggested that treatment with recombinant human basic FGF (rhbFGF) could promote re-epithelialisation in acute wounds (Mazue et al, 1991), later randomised placebo-controlled studies of pressure sores (Robson et al, 1992c) and diabetic foot ulcers (Richard et al, 1995) showed that chronic wounds may be comparatively less reponsive. In view of information from studies to date, and in view of the knowledge that bFGF activity is repressed under hypoxic conditions (Wu et al, 1995), this growth factor appears to be a weak candidate for commercial development as a chronic wound therapy.

Platelet-derived growth factor (PDGF)

First isolated from platelets, but now known to be produced by a variety of cells, PDGF is primarily recognised for its role as a potent mitogen for fibroblasts, endothelial cells and smooth muscle cells. In addition to promoting cellular proliferation PDGF is thought to be centrally involved in the chemotaxis of monocytes, neutrophils and fibroblasts, matrix synthesis and matrix remodelling (Pierce et al, 1991).

Accelerated repair in response to the application of PDGF has been reported in a variety of animal models. PDGF has been shown to promote: angiogenesis, re-epithelialisation and granulation tissue formation in excisional wounds, and improved breaking strength in incisional wounds (Pierce et al, 1989; 1991). It has also been found to reverse the healing defects associated with diabetes (Grotendorst et al, 1985; Greenhalgh et al, 1990); ischaemia (Mustoe et al, 1994a) and radiation (Mustoe et al, 1989).

Of all the growth factors studied to date PDGF has received most attention, with six published clinical trials since 1992. To varying degrees all have suggested that PDGF treatment accelerates repair in chronic wounds. Initial studies performed on hospitalised paraplegics with pressure sores reported promising though statistically insignificant effects (Robson et al, 1992a b).

Subsequent studies on elderly patients with grade III/IV pressure sores reported significantly accelerated wound closure (Mustoe et al, 1994b); an observation which was later explained in terms of enhanced fibroblast recruitment, angiogenesis and collagen fibre formation in biopsies taken from PDGF treated sores (Pierce et al, 1994).

The ability of rhPDGF-BB to promote repair in chronic diabetic wounds has recently been asserted by several large multi-centre randomised placebo controlled trials (Steed et al, 1995; Wieman et al, 1998; d'Hemecourt et al, 1998). In recognition of these supporting clinical studies, rhPDGF-BB, in the form of Becalpermin, became the first recombinant growth factor preparation to be approved by the US Food and Drug Administration for use on lower-extremity diabetic neuropathic ulcers.

In agreement with earlier work by Mustoe et al, (1994b), the commercial preparation Becalpermin has also been reported to accelerate pressure sore healing significantly (Rees et al, 1998). Taking all published data into consideration, and in view of the fact that certain chronic wounds have been found to be PDGF deficient (Cooper et al, 1994; Pierce et al, 1995), it would appear that PDGF may be a significant player in future of growth factor therapy.

Transforming growth factor-β (TGF-β)

There are three forms of TGF-β in mammals (TGF-β1, 2 and 3), of which TGF-β1 is the best characterised. TGF-β is known for its roles in fibrosis and immuno-suppression. *In vitro* studies have demonstrated that TGF-β can influence, and may consequently be involved with, many wound healing processes. TGF-β has been found to:

▶ be chemotactic to monocytes and fibroblasts

▶ promote extracellular matrix synthesis

▶ inhibit the synthesis of matrix degrading protease

▶ regulate growth factor synthesis by a variety of cells (O'Kane and Ferguson, 1997)

Accelerated repair in response to TGF-β has been demonstrated in a variety of normal and impaired animals (Bernstein et al, 1991; Beck et al, 1991) following both topical application after injury and systemic administration prior to injury (Beck et al, 1993).

Few clinical investigations involving TGF-β have been reported to date. This is primarily due to concern over the induction of inappropriate fibrotic or immuno-suppressive responses, rather than a lack of awareness of the central role that TFG-β plays in tissue repair. Two trials investigating the application of bovine bone derived TGF-β2 to chronic ulcers were published in 1995.

One (Robson et al, 1995a) demonstrated a significant improvement in the rate of ulcer closure, whereas the other (Robson et al, 1995b) showed a trend towards accelerated venous ulcer repair but no statistically significant improvement. As it has been reported that human chronic wounds, specifically pressure sores, are TGF-β1 deficient (Schmid et al, 1993); the results of ongoing and future trials involving TGF-β are eagerly awaited.

Epidermal growth factor (EGF)

Epidermal growth factor (EGF), the first growth factor to be described in the scientific literature, is produced during wound repair by various cells including platelets, keratinocytes and activated macrophages (Schultz et al, 1991). Studies of partial thickness burns and skin graft donor sites in animals demonstrated that treatment with EGF significantly accelerated epidermal regeneration (Brown et al, 1986). EGF has also been found to promote dermal proliferation in partial thickness wounds, improve tensile strength in surgical incisions (Brown et al, 1988) and correct the delay in healing associated with diabetes (Hennessey et al, 1990).

The first reported clinical study investigating rhEGF on wound repair involved its application to skin graft donor sites (Brown et al, 1989). rhEGF supplementation was found significantly to reduce the time to complete epidermal regeneration. The observation that exogenous rhEGF could accelerate normal repair encouraged further investigation into its ability to promote repair in chronic wounds. Brown et al, (1991) reported that while no evidence of healing was observed during treatment with silver sulphadiazine alone, subsequent treatment of these wounds with EGF-supplemented cream resulted in wound closure in eight out of nine patients after approximately one month. In the above cross-over study, the possibility exists that continued treatment with silver sulphadiazine cream without EGF supplementation would have resulted in similar levels of wound closure.

Results of the only reported randomised placebo-controlled clinical trial of rhEGF on chronic wounds were encouraging, but no significant benefit, in terms of numbers of wounds healed or speed of repair, was associated with rhEGF treatment (Falanga et al, 1992). The reputation of exogenous rhEGF as a prospective wound stimulatory agent was further damaged when it was reported that placebo-treated partial thickness wounds made in healthy volunteers heal at a rate indistinguishable from that of similar wounds treated with rhEGF (Cohen et al, 1995).

In general terms, there is at present little data to support the use of this growth factor in the treatment of non-healing or slow-to-heal wounds, although accelerated repair of acute injuries remains a possibility.

Interleukin-1 (IL-1)

Interleukin-1 (IL-1), which can exist in two forms (IL-1α and IL-1β), is produced by a variety of cell types involved in the wound repair process, including monocytes, macrophages, fibroblasts, endothelial cells and keratinocytes. Although not widely studied in terms of wound healing, IL-1 is known to be involved with many processes associated with inflammation and tissue repair including activation and chemotaxis of neutrophils and macrophages, fibroblast and keratinocyte proliferation, angiogenesis, matrix synthesis and collagenase production. Treatment with IL-1 has been shown to accelerate repair in several animal models including that in radiation-impaired mice (Vegesna et al, 1995).

There are currently only two published clinical studies in which the effect of IL-1 on wound repair has been investigated. The first reported that rhIL-1β treatment significantly reduced the time to complete healing compared with placebo treatment (Holt et al, 1991). Whereas the second reported that rhIL-1β, had no effect on wound healing (Robson et al, 1994). Dose levels in these studies were kept low owing to fears over adverse reactions to treatment. As no such reactions were observed the authors suggested that higher doses, similar to those used in other growth factor studies, may prove effective in subsequent trials.

Platelet-derived wound healing formula (PDWHF)

The most extensively studied growth factor preparation in wound healing research is PDWHF, a formulation produced by degranulating platelets with thrombin. PDWHF has been shown to contain low concentrations of several wound-healing-associated growth factors (Holloway, 1993). The effect of both autologous (patients own platelets) and homologous (donor platelets) PDWHF preparations have been studied. The risk of transfer of blood borne pathogens, from blood donor to PDWHF recipient, in the use of homologous platelet preparations is a serious ongoing concern.

In 1986, Knighton et al published the first clinical study investigating PDWHF on wound repair. This uncontrolled trial suggested that treatment with PDWHF (derived from autologous platelets) was an effective therapy with which to treat a variety of chronic non-healing wounds. Atri et al (1990) also reported beneficial effects in an uncontrolled study using an homologous platelet preparation, derived from the blood of healthy volunteers.

The validity of these first two studies has been questioned over the lack of appropriate control treatments. In a later placebo-controlled trial re-epithelialisation was found to be significantly more rapid following autologous PDWHF treatment than was observed following treatment with a placebo (Knighton et al, 1990).

Disagreeing with all that had gone before, Krupski et al (1991) reported that treatment with autologous PDWHF in a controlled trial was at best ineffective and at worst may have actually delayed repair. This report, which represented the results from a single centre in a larger, as yet unreported, commercially sponsored multi-centre clinical trial, elicited a passionate dismissive response from those associated with the development of PDWHF as a commercial wound healing product (Dosick, 1991; Loss et al, 1991; Glover et al, 1991).

The ability of a commercially prepared homologous platelet preparation, CT-102 APST (Curative Technologies, Setauket, NY, USA), to influence the repair of diabetic foot ulcers was investigated by Steed et al (1992). Based on reduction in both wound volume and area, CT-102 APST was found significantly to accelerate wound closure relative to placebo treatment.

The most recently reported randomised placebo-controlled trial of PDWHF involved the study of CT-102 APST in diabetic foot ulcer patients (Holloway et al, 1993). In this study, 80% of treated ulcers healed in the 20-week study period; whereas only 29% of saline placebo-treated wounds were found to heal. Those groups that have reported benefit in using PDWHF invariably indicate that this preparation must be used in the context of a comprehensive and holistic wound care approach.

Comment

With the exception of trials of PDWHF, all other clinical studies to date have investigated the effects of single growth factor preparations. Normal wound repair is, however, known to involve the production, action and interaction of many growth factors. A more appropriate and effective approach may involve the combined use of several growth factors with complementary activity.

Support for such an approach comes from various pre-clinical studies using healing-impaired diabetic mice. In these studies synergistic effects on wound closure have been observed following treatment with PDGF in combination with both TGF-α (Brown et al, 1994) and insulin-like growth factor-II (IGF-II) (Greenhalgh et al, 1993). Other growth factor combinations such as PDGF-BB and insulin-like growth factor-I (IGF-I) have been found to be more effective than PDGF-BB alone in promoting repair in elderly diabetic mice (Kiritsy et al, 1995). Growth factor combination may be unnecessary if a given growth factor could induce production of other complementary growth factors within the wound site.

From clinical investigations performed to date it would appear that chronic wounds vary in their response to growth factor application and a proportion are effectively non-responsive (Pierce et al 1994). Growth factor therapy would be much more attractive if it were possible to differentiate between growth factor responsive and unresponsive wounds. Such patient pre-selection would reduce growth factor wastage and make growth factor therapy more cost-effective.

There are a number of reasons why the application of a growth factor may fail to elicit the desired stimulatory effect on wound repair. As many wounds do respond, this lack of effect is unlikely to be associated with the growth factor or the form in which it is presented but, rather, with the tissues being treated.

In order for a specific growth factor to elicit a response within a cell, the target cell must both bear appropriate growth factor receptors and have intact intracellular signal transduction pathways. It is possible that growth factor non-responsive wounds are populated with effector cells that are growth factor receptor, or perhaps even signal transduction pathway, defective/deficient, although this has yet to be investigated to any significant degree.

More plausible explanations for this lack of responsiveness to growth factor therapy are based on the environment in which the introduced growth factors are asked to work (that is, the chronic wound environment).

A large proportion of chronic wounds are characterised by ischaemic hypoxia. It is known that certain key wound healing cell types, such as macrophages, respond to such hypoxic environments by producing a variety of growth factors during the normal repair process (Kuwabara et al, 1995). It is also apparent that certain growth factors function better than others under such conditions. Fibroblast growth factor-4 (FGF-4), for example, is apparently active in hypoxic environments, whereas the activity of bFGF (FGF-2), a related growth factor, is severely impeded under such conditions (Wu et al, 1995).

Such observations suggest that the current, largely speculative, approach to growth factor selection should be replaced with a more measured approach based on both wound pathophysiology and growth factor characteristics.

While much is known about chronic wound pathophysiology, more has yet to be learnt. It has been suggested that new tissue generation is prevented in chronic wounds by the presence of high levels of protein digesting enzymes (proteases), low levels of protease inhibitors, or a combination of both. In order for both endogenous and applied growth factors to initiate and promote repair, they and their receptors must remain stable in the chronic wound environment.

Recent work suggests that stability is compromised in chronic wounds. Studies by Yager et al (1997) and Eming et al (1998) have shown certain growth factors, specifically TGF-b1, PDGF-BB and vascular endothelial cell growth factor (VEGF), are rapidly degraded by wound fluid from some chronic wounds. Interestingly, this degradation can be significantly reduced by adding protease inhibitors to wound fluid, specifically those that inhibit neutrophil elastase. This observation strongly implicates this protease both in the degradation of applied growth factors and wound chronicity as a whole.

With early work suggesting that protease inhibitors could protect EGF and promote its effects on wound repair in animals (Kiyohara et al, 1991), it is not surprising that a great deal of effort is currently being directed towards the development and testing of various novel protease inhibitors, both as stand-alone therapies and as an adjunct to growth factor therapy.

It is, however, important to note that complete protease ablation in chronic wounds is far from desirable, as various proteases are essential to the repair process. They are involved in activities such as fibrinolysis, the release of matrix bound growth factors (Whitelock et al, 1996), cellular migration and matrix remodelling.

Growth factor protection and stabilisation can be achieved by means other than by protease inhibitors. Recent work has suggested that certain materials such as derivatised dextrans (Meddahi et al, 1996) are able to limit protease-associated growth factor damage. These and other materials, which bind and protect growth factors without limiting their availability within a wound, may prove useful as vehicles for growth factor delivery.

The removal of dead and devitalised tissue, debridement, is widely believed to be central to effective wound management. Debridement can be achieved by a variety of means, including enzymatic methods. Enzymes used are proteases which are capable of digesting a variety of proteins including growth factors. In order to reduce the likelihood of enzymatic damage, growth factor application is best commenced after debridement or conducted using enzymes that do not affect growth factor activity (Gosiewska et al, 1998).

Clearly any factor that modulates the ability of cells to respond to a given growth factor may result in a change of responsiveness of a tissue to growth factor treatment. Factors known to influence cellular responsiveness to growth factors include certain drugs such as glucocorticoids and cyclosporin-A (Ahuja et al, 1995; Brauchle et al, 1995; Frank et al, 1996; Tang and Gilchrist, 1996). A more detailed and extensive consideration of factors capable of confounding growth factor activity may well result in improved patient/wound responsiveness to treatment.

As with any other aspect of medical care, safety is a major overriding consideration in the therapeutic development of growth factors. The various safety fears, including antibody production against introduced growth factors and inappropriate fibrosis, have yet to be realised. Tumour growth is known to result from the inappropriate expression of various growth factors, many of which have been found to be involved in wound repair.

The possibility exists that the application of growth factors by systemic, local or topical routes may promote tumourigenesis. Sustained and uncontrolled (tumour-like) growth in response to growth factor therapy has yet to be reported in the clinical wound healing literature, although work in animals suggest that this possibility may be real (Siewecke et al, 1990; Reinbach et al, 1995; Hofer et al, 1998).

A variety of conditions such as age, diabetes and various forms of medical treatment (such as radio- and chemotherapy) are known to give rise to wound healing deficiencies. Animal studies investigating the possibility that wounds can be primed to heal more effectively by introducing growth factors into the wound site prior to surgery have recently been reported (Desai et al, 1997).

Priming of acute surgical incision sites with PDGF-AB one day prior to injury has been found to accelerate macrophage recruitment, cellular proliferation and the gain of wound strength after injury. Growth factor-based wound priming, although yet to be tested clinically, may be particularly useful for elective surgery patients prone to delayed or defective wound repair.

Several new techniques designed to introduce growth factors to wounds are currently under development. Gene therapy, which in this setting is the introduction of growth factor genes into cells residing within a wound, is receiving some attention in the scientific literature (Eming et al, 1997). This technique has recently been used to accelerate repair in diabetic mice following transfection of the human aFGF (FGF-1) gene (Sun et al, 1997). Although in its infancy with regard to wound healing, gene therapy is much more established in other areas of medicine (Hess, 1996).

Other less complicated techniques include the introduction of immunomodulatory agents, such as glucan phosphate, which promote the activity of growth factor-producing cells within the wound (Portera et al, 1997). Some established treatments, such as zinc oxide, have been reported to increase growth factor synthesis (Tarnow et al, 1994) which may explain their ability to promote repair in certain chronic wounds. An approach by which cells within the wound are encouraged to produce their own growth factors is intrinsically, and no doubt financially, a more attractive option than the application of expensive pre-synthesised factors.

The technology underlying commercial growth factor production is complex, and manufacturing costs are high. As growth factor therapy is still in its infancy cost-effectiveness has yet to be established or indeed considered. With an appreciation of the current declines and restrictions in health budgets, future clinical trials may benefit from including endpoints that reflect financial as well as therapeutic consequences of growth factor use.

Growth factor preparation	Wound	Study type	Growth factor concentration	Patient number	Reported outcome	Reference
PDWHF	CWV	NC	Not known (variable)	49	Effective	Knighton et al, 1986
rhEGF	AW	R, PC, DB	Applied in cream at 10μg/ml	12	Effective	Brown et al, 1989
PGF	VU	R, PC, DB	Gel dressing soaked in PGF solution 26 μg/cm²	18	Effective	Burgos et al, 1989
PDWHF – homologous	CWV	CO-NC	Not known (variable)	23	Effective	Atri et al, 1990
PDWHF	CWV	R, PC, CO	Not known (variable)	32	Effective	Knighton et al, 1990
rhIL-1β	AW	R, PC, DB	0.1, 0.5 or 1μg /wound/day	36	Effective	Holt et al, 1991
rhbFGF	AW	R, PC	0.5*g/blister	24	Effective	Masue et al, 1991
PDWHF	CWV	R, PC, DB	Not known (variable)	18	No benefit	Krupski et al, 1991
rhEGF	CWV	CO	Applied in cream at 10μg /g	9	Effective	Brown et al, 1991
PDWHF (CT-102) *1	DFU	R, PC, DB	Not known (variable)	13	Effective	Steed et al, 1992
rhPDGF-BB	PS/U	R, PC, DB	0.01, 0.1 or 1μg/cm² wound area	20	Limited benefit	Robson et al, 1992a; b
rhbFGF	PS/U	R, PC, B	1, 5 or 10μg/ cm² wound area	50	Effective	Robson et al, 1992c
rhEGF	VU	R,PC, DB	10μg/ml	44	Limited benefit	Falanga et al, 1992
PDWHF (CT-102) *1	DFU	R, PC	Not known (variable)	70	Effective	Holloway et al, 1993
rhPDGF-BB	PS/U	R, PC, DB	1 or 3μg/cm² wound area	41	Effective	Mustoe et al, 1994b
rhIL-1β	PS/U	R, PC, DB	0.01, 0.1 or 1μg/cm²	26	No benefit	Robson et al, 1994
TGF-β2 – bovine bone	VU	PC, O	0.5μg/cm² wound area	12	Effective	Robson et al, 1995
TGF-β2 – bovine bone	VU	R, PC, DB	2.5μg/cm² 3 times per week	36	Limited benefit	Robson et al, 1995
rhbFGF	DFU	R, PC, DB	0.25–0.75μg/cm²	17	No benefit	Richard et al, 1995
EGF	AW-PT	PC	Not stated	17	No benefit	Cohen et al, 1995
rhPDGF-BB	DFU	R, PC, DB	2.2μg/cm² wound area	118	Effective	Steed et al, 1995; 1996
rhPDGF-BB *2	DFU	R, PC, DB	100–300ug per gram of gel	382	Effective	Wieman et al, 1998
rhPDGF-BB *2	DFU	R, SB	100μg per gram of gel	172	Limited benefit	d'Hemecourt et al, 1998
rhPDGF-BB *2	PS/U	R, PC, DB	100–300ug per gram of gel	124	Effective	Rees et al, 1998

Table 2 Reported clinical studies investigating the effect of growth factor preparations on dermal wound repair

Key: *1 Curative Technologies, USA; *2 Regranex* (becalpermin) Gel (Ortho-McNeil Pharmaceutical, USA). PGF – placental growth factor preparation
AW – acute wounds; DB – double blind; CO – cross over trial; CWV – chronic wounds various; DFU – diabetic foot ulcers; R – randomised; PC – placebo controlled; VU – venous ulcers.
NC – non-controlled; PS/U pressure sores/ulcers; PT – partial thickness; R – randomised; PC – placebo controlled; VU – venous ulcers.

References

Ahuja, S.S. et al (1995) Regulation of transforming growth factor-beta(1) and its receptor by cyclosporine in human T-lymphocytes. *Transplantation;* 60: 7, 718–723.

Atri, S.C. et al (1990) Use of homologous platelet factors in achieving total healing of recalcitrant skin ulcers. *Surgery;* 108: 3, 508–512.

Beck, L.S. et al (1991) TGF-beta 1 accelerates wound healing: reversal of steroid-impaired healing in rats and rabbits. *Growth Factors;* 5: 4, 295–304.

Beck, L.S. et al (1993) One systemic administration of transforming growth factor-beta 1 reverses age- or glucocorticoid-impaired wound healing. *Journal of Clinical Investigations;* 92: 6, 2841–2849.

Bernstein, E.F. et al (1991) Transforming growth factor-beta improves healing of radiation-impaired wounds. *Journal of Investigative Dermatology;* 97: 3, 430–434.

Bosenberg, M.W., Massague, J. (1993) Juxtacrine cell signaling molecules. *Current Opinions on Cellular Biology;* 5: 5, 832–838.

Brauchle, M. et al (1995) Suppression of keratinocyte growth factor expression by glucocorticoids *in vitro* and during wound-healing. *Journal of Investigative Dermatology;* 105: 4, 579–584.

Broadley, K.N. et al (1989) Specific antibodies implicate basic fibroblast growth factor in normal wound repair. *Laboratory Investigations;* 61: 571–575.

Brown, G.L. et al (1986) Enhancement of epidermal regeneration by biosynthetic epidermal growth factor. *Journal of Experimental Medicine;* 163: 5, 1319–1324.

Brown, G.L. et al (1988) Acceleration of tensile strength of incisions treated with EGF and TGF-beta. *Annals of Surgery;* 208: 6, 788–794.

Brown, G.L. et al (1989) Enhancement of wound healing by topical treatment with epidermal growth factor. *New England Journal of Medicine;* 321: 2, 76–79.

Brown, G.L. et al (1991). Stimulation of healing of chronic wounds by epidermal growth factor. *Plastic Reconstructive Surgery;* 88: 2, 189–194.

Brown, R.L. et al (1994) PDGF and TGF-alpha act synergistically to improve wound healing in the genetically diabetic mouse. *Journal of Surgical Results;* 56: 562–570.

Burgos, H. et al (1989) Placental angiogenic and growth factors in the treatment of chronic varicose ulcers: preliminary communication. *Journal of the Royal Society of Medicine;* 82; 10, 598–599.

Cohen, I.K. et al (1995) Topical application of epidermal growth factor onto partial-thickness wounds in human volunteers does not enhance reepithelialization. *Plastic Reconstructive Surgery;* 96; 2, 251–254.

Cooper, D.M. et al (1994) determination of endogenous cytokines in chronic wounds. *Annals of Surgery;* 219: 6, 688–692.

Dellaert, M.M. et al (1997) Influence of topical human epidermal growth factor on postkeratoplasty re-epithelialisation. *British Journal of Ophthalmology;* 81: 5, 391–395.

Desai, H. et al (1997) Growth factor priming and wound repair (abstract). Seventh Annual Meeting of the European Tissue Repair Society, Koln, Germany. *Wound Repair and Regeneration;* 5: 1.

d'Hemecourt, P.A. et al (1998) Sodium carboxymethylcellulaose aqueous-based gel vs. becalpermin in patients with non-healing lower extremity diabetic ulcers. *Wounds;* 10: 3, 69–75.

Dosick, S.M. (1992) A prospective randomized trial of autologous platelet-derived wound healing factors for treatment of chronic nonhealing wounds: a preliminary report. *Journal of Vascular Surgery;* 16: 1, 125–8.

Eming, S.A. et al (1997) Gene therapy for tissue repair: approaches and prospects. *British Journal of Plastic Surgery;* 50: 7, 491–500.

Eming, S.A. et al (1998). Protealysis of VEGF in chronic non-healing wounds (abstract). Proceedings of the Eighth Annual Meeting of the European Tissue Repair Society, Copenhagen, Denmark; 27–30.

Falanga, V. et al (1992) Topical use of human recombinant epidermal growth factor (h-EGF) in venous ulcers. *Journal of Dermatological and Surgical Oncology;* 18: 7, 604–606.

Fina, M. et al (1991) Improved healing of tympanic membrane perforations with basic fibroblast growth factor. *Growth Factors;* 5: 4, 265–272.

Frank, S. et al (1996) Transforming growth factors beta 1, beta 2, and beta 3 and their receptors are differentially regulated during normal and impaired wound healing. *Journal of Biology and Chemistry;* 271: 17, 10188–10193.

Geilen, C.C. et al (1996) The mitogen-activated protein kinases system (MAP kinase cascade): its role in skin signal transduction. A review. *Journal of Dermatological Science* 12: 3, 255–262.

Girdler, N.M. et al (1995) The effect of epidermal growth factor mouthwash on cytotoxic-induced oral ulceration. A phase I clinical trial. *American Journal of Clinical Oncology;* 18: 5, 403–406.

Gosiewska, A. et al (1998) The effect of enzymatic debriders on the biological activity of becalpermin (rhPDGF-BB), the active agent of Regranex (becalpermin) gel. Proceedings of the Eighth Annual Meeting of the European Tissue Repair Society, Copenhagen, Denmark; 27–30.

Greenhalgh, D.G. et al (1990) PDGF and FGF stimulate wound healing in the genetically diabetic mouse. *American Journal of Pathology;* 136: 1235–1250.

Greenhalgh, D.G. et al (1993) Synergistic actions of platelet derived growth factor and the insulin like growth factors *in vivo*: enhancement of tissue repair in genetically diabetic mice. *Wound Repair and Regeneration;* 1: 69–81.

Grotendorst, G.R. et al (1985) Stimulation of granulation tissue formation by platelet-derived growth factor in normal and diabetic rats. *Journal of Clinical Investigations;* 76: 6, 2323–2329.

Hart, C.E. et al (1990) Purification of PDGF-AB and PDGF-BB from human platelets and identification of all three dimers in human platelets. *Biochemistry;* 29; 1, 166–172.

Hennessey, P.J. et al (1990) EGF increases short-term type I collagen accumulation during wound healing in diabetic rats. *Journal of Pediatric Surgery;* 25: 8, 893–897.

Hess, P, (1996) Gene therapy: a brief review. *Clinical Laboratory Medicine;* 16: 1, 197–211.

Hofer, S.O. et al (1998) Wound-induced tumour progression: a probable role in recurrence after tumour resection. *Archives of Surgery;* 133: 4, 383–389.

Holloway, G.A. et al (1993) A randomised controlled dose response trial of activated platelet supernatent topical CT-102 (APST) in chronic non-healing wounds in patients with diabetes mellitus. *Wounds;* 5: 198–206

Holt, D.R. et al (1991) Recombinant human IL-1b enhances human wound epithelialisation. *Surgical Forum;* 42: 3–4.

Howell, T.H. et al (1997) A phase I/II clinical trial to evaluate a combination of recombinant human platelet-derived growth factor-BB and recombinant human insulin-like growth factor-I in patients with periodontal disease. *Journal of Periodontology;* 68: 12, 1186–93.

Knighton, D.R. et al (1986) Classification and treatment of chronic nonhealing wounds: Successful treatment with autologous platelet-derived wound healing factors (PDWHF). *Annals of Surgery;* 204: 3, 322–330.

Knighton, D.R. et al (1990) Stimulation of repair in chronic, nonhealing, cutaneous ulcers using platelet-derived wound healing formula. *Surgery, Gynecology and Obstetrics;* 170: 1, 56–60.

Kiritsy, C.P. et al (1995) Combination of platelet derived growth factor-BB and insulin like growth factor-I is more effective at stimulating complete healing of full thickness wounds in older diabetic mice. *Wound Repair and Regeneration;* 3: 340–350.

Kiyohara, Y. et al (1991) Improvement in wound healing by epidermal growth factor (EGF) ointment: II. Effect of protease inhibitor. nafamostat, on stabilisation and efficacy of EGF in burn. *Journal of Pharmacobiodynamics;* 14: 47 –52.

Krupski, W.C. et al. A prospective randomized trial of autologous platelet-derived wound healing factors for treatment of chronic nonhealing wounds: a preliminary report. *Journal of Vascular Surgery;* 14: 4, 526–32.

Kuwabara, K et al (1995) Hypoxia-mediated induction of acidic/basic fibroblast growth factor and platelet-derived growth factor in mononuclear phagocytes stimulates growth of hypoxic endothelial cells. *Proceedings of the National Academy of Science. (USA);* 92: 10, 4606–4610.

Matsue, G. et al (1991) Preclinical and clinical studies with recombinant human basic fibroblast growth factor. *Annals of the New York Academy of Sciences;* 638: 329–340.

Maciag, T. et al, (1994) Novel mechanisms of fibroblast growth factor 1 function. *Recent Progress in Hormone Research;* 49: 105–123.

McGee, G.S. et al (1988) Recombinant basic fibroblast growth factor accelerates wound healing. *Journal of Surgical Research;* 45: 1, 145–153.

Meddahi, A. et al (1996) FGF protection and inhibition of human neutrophil elastase by carboxymethyl benzylamide sulfonate dextran derivatives. *International Journal of Biological Macromolecules;* 18: 1–2, 141–145.

Mondain, M. et al (1995) Neutralizing antibodies against basic fibroblast growth factor influence the healing of traumatic tympanic membrane perforations. *ORL; Journal of Oto-Rhino-Laryngology & its Related Specialities;* 57: 1, 28–32.

Mustoe, T.A. et al (1987). Accelerated healing of incisional wounds in rats induced by transforming growth factor type b. *Science;* 347: 1333–1336.

Mustoe, T.A. et al (1989) Reversal of impaired wound healing in irradiated rats by platelet derived growth factor-BB: requirement of an active bone marrow. *American Journal of Surgery;* 158: 4, 345–350.

Mustoe, T.A. et al (1994a) The effect of hypoxia on growth factor actions: differential response of basic fibroblast growth factor and platelet derived growth factor in an ischemic wound model. *Wound Repair and Regeneration;* 2: 277–283.

Mustoe, T.A. et al (1994b). A phase II study to evaluate recombinant platelet-derived growth factor-BB in the treatment of stage 3 and 4 pressure ulcers. *Archives of Surgery;* 129: 2, 213–219.

O'Kane, S. and Ferguson, M.W. (1997) Transforming growth factor beta s and wound healing. *International Journal of Biochemical and Cellular Biology;* 29: 1, 63–78.

Pierce, G.F. et al (1989) Transforming growth factor b reverses the wound healing deficit caused by systemic glucocorticoid administration: possible regulation in macrophages by platelet derived growth factor. *Proceedings of the National Academy of Science. (USA);* 86: 7, 2229–2233.

Pierce, G.F. et al (1989) Platelet-derived growth factor and transforming growth factor-beta enhance tissue repair activities by unique mechanisms. *Journal of Cellular Biology;* 109: 1, 429–440.

Pierce, G.F. et al (1991) Role of platelet-derived growth factor in wound healing. *International Journal of Cellular Biochemistry;* 45: 4, 319–326.

Pierce, G.F. et al (1992) Platelet-derived growth factor (BB homodimer), transforming growth factor-beta 1, and basic fibroblast growth factor in dermal wound healing: neovessel and matrix formation and cessation of repair. *American Journal of Pathology;* 140: 6, 1375–1388.

Pierce, G.F. et al (1994). Tissue repair processes in healing chronic pressure ulcers treated with recombinant platelet-derived growth factor BB. *American Journal of Pathology;* 145: 6, 1399–1410.

Pierce, G.F. et al (1995) Detection of platelet-derived growth factor (PDGF)-AA in actively healing human wounds treated with recombinant PDGF-BB and absence of PDGF in chronic nonhealing wounds. *Journal of Clinical Investigations;* 96: 3, 1336–1350.

Plemons, J.M. et al (1996). PDGF-B producing cells and PDGF-B gene expression in normal gingiva and cyclosporine A-induced gingival overgrowth. *Journal of Periodontology;* 67: 3, 264–270.

Rees, R.S. et al (1988) Becalpermin gel in the treatment of pressure ulcers: A randomised, double blind, placebo controlled study (abstract). Eighth Annual Meeting of the European Tissue Repair Society. Copenhagen, Denmark. 1998.

Reinbach, D. et al (1995) Collagen promotes perianastomotic tumor-growth in an experimental animal-model. *Journal of Surgical Oncology;* 60: 2, 112–115.

Reuterdahl, C. et al (1993) Tissue localisation of b-receptors for platelet-derived growth factor and platelet-derived growth factor B chain during wound repair in humans. *Journal of Clinical Investigations;* 91: 5, 2065–2075.

Richard, J.L. et al (1995) Effect of topical basic fibroblast growth factor on the healing of chronic diabetic neuropathic ulcer of the foot. A pilot, randomized, double-blind, placebo-controlled study. *Diabetes Care;* 18: 1, 64–69.

Robson, M.C. et al (1992a) Platelet-derived growth factor BB for the treatment of chronic pressure ulcers. *Lancet;* 339: 8784, 23–25.

Robson, M.C. et al (1992b) Recombinant human platelet-derived growth factor-BB for the treatment of chronic pressure ulcers, *Annals of Plastic Surgery;* 29: 3, 193–201.

Robson, M.C. et al (1992c) The safety and effect of topically applied recombinant basic fibroblast growth factor on the healing of chronic pressure sores. *Annals of Surgery;* 216: 4, 401–406.

Robson, M.C. et al (1994) Safety and effect of topical recombinant interleukin-1b in the management of pressure sores. *Wound Repair and Regeneration;* 2: 177–81.

Robson, M.C. et al (1995) Safelt and effect of transforming growth factor-b2 for treatment of venous stasis ulcers. *Wound Repair and Regeneration;* 3: 157–167

Schmid, P. et al (1993) TGF-beta s and TGF-beta type II receptor in human epidermis: differential expression in acute and chronic skin wounds. *Journal of Pathology;* 171: 3, 191–7.

Shukla, A. et al (1998) Differential expression of proteins during healing of cutaneous wounds in experimental normal and chronic models. *Biochemical and Biophysical Research Communications;* 244: 2, 434–439.

Schultz, G.S. et al (1987) Epithelial wound healing enhanced by transforming growth factor-alpha and vaccinia growth factor. *Science;* 235: 4786, 350–352.

Schultz, G. et al (1991) EGF and TGF-alpha in wound healing and repair. *Journal of Cellular Biochemistry;* 45: 4, 346–352.

Siewecke, M.H. et al (1990) Mediation of wound related Rous sarcoma virus tumourigenesis by TGF-b. *Science;* 248: 1656–1660.

Steed, D.L. et al (1992) Randomized prospective double-blind trial in healing chronic diabetic foot ulcers: CT-102 activated platelet supernatant, topical versus placebo. *Diabetes Care;* 15: 11, 1598–1604.

Steed, D.L. and the Diabetic Ulcer Study Group (1995) Clinical evaluation of recombinant human platelet-derived growth factor for the treatment of lower extremity diabetic ulcers. Diabetic Ulcer Study Group. *Journal of Vascular Surgery;* 21: 1, 71–78.

Sun, L. et al (1997) Transfection with aFGF cDNA improves wound healing. *Journal of Investigative Dermatology;* 108: 3, 313–318.

Tanaka, E. et al (1996) Mechanism of acceleration of wound healing by basic fibroblast growth factor in genetically diabetic mice. *Biological and Pharmaceutical Bulletin;* 19: 9, 1141–1148.

Tang, A.M. and Gilchrest BA (1996) Regulation of keratinocyte growth factor gene expression in human skin fibroblasts. *Journal of Dermatological Science;* 11: 1, 41–50.

Tarnow, P. et al (1995) Topical zinc-oxide treatment increases endogenous gene-expression of insulin-like growth-factor-I in granulation- tissue from porcine wounds. *Scandinavian Journal of Plastic Reconstructive Surgery and Hand Surgery;* 28: 4, 255–259.

Werner, S. et al (1992). Large induction of keratinocyte growth factor expression in the dermis during wound healing. *Proceedings of the National Academy of Science. (USA);* 89: 15, 6896–6900.

Whitelock, J.M. et al (1996) The degradation of human endothelial cell-derived perlecan and release of bound basic fibroblast growth factor by stromelysin, collagenase, plasmin, and heparanases. *Journal of Biological Chemistry;* 271: 17, 10079–10086.

Wieman, T.J. et al (1998). Efficacy and safety of a topical gel formulation of recombinant human platelet-derived growth factor-BB (becaplermin) in patients with chronic neuropathic diabetic ulcers. A phase III randomized placebo-controlled double-blind study. *Diabetes Care;* 21: 5, 822–827.

Wu, L. et al (1995). Effects of oxygen on wound responses to growth factors: Kaposi's FGF, but not basic FGF stimulates repair in ischemic wounds. *Growth Factors;* 12: 1, 29–35.

Yager, D.E. et al (1997). Ability of chronic wound fluids to degrade peptide growth factors is associated with increased levels of elastase activity and diminished level of protease inhibitors. *Wound Repair and Regeneration;* 5: 23–32.

16 Glossary

Keith Cutting

Thirty-degree tilt technique	The positioning of patients so that risk of pressure sore development is decreased. The patient is placed in a laterally inclined position, supported with pillows, with their back making a 30-degree angle with the support surface
ABPI	See ankle brachial pressure index
Abscess	A local collection of necrotic tissue, bacteria and white cells known as pus. This collection of infection is retained within a wall formed of phagocytes and strands of fibrin
Anaerobes	Obligate anaerobes are bacteria that do not tolerate free oxygen and grow where there is no air or where there is a low oxidation-reduction potential, for instance, *Clostridium perfringens*, *Bacteroides fragilis*
Angiogenesis	The generation of new blood vessels initially seen at the base of a wound
Ankle brachial pressure index (ABPI)	A Doppler ultrasound test used to determine the presence and degree of peripheral arterial disease in patients with leg ulcers
Ankle flare	Distension of the small vessels which appears around the ankle and heel and is associated with varicose vein formation, venous hypertension and venous ulceration
Autolysis	The breakdown of devitalised tissue by leucocytes
Bacteroides	Anaerobic Gram-negative bacillus normally found in the oro-pharynx and also in faeces. In wound infections it is usually regarded as an opportunist organism

Callus	A build-up of keratinised skin. This is a reaction to persistent pressure
Cavitation	The generation of a temporary cavity as a result of a high-velocity missile (bullet) entering soft tissue
Cellulitis	A spreading non-suppurative infection of the soft tissue
Collagen	A protein generated by fibroblasts which provides the supportive network of connective tissue
Colonisation	Multiplication of micro-organisms without a corresponding host reaction
Commensals	Micro-organisms which do not react with their host, that is, they are non-pathogenic and become part of the host's normal flora
Complement (C)	A complex group of proteins and other factors found in serum and other body fluids which are normally inactive
Contamination	Presence of micro-organisms but without their multiplication
Contraction	A function of the healing process in granulating wounds whereby the edges of the wound are drawn towards each other
Cytokine	A chemical messenger – see also growth factors
Debridement	The removal of devitalised tissue and foreign matter from a wound
Doppler ultrasound	Used to record the ankle brachial pressure index (see ankle brachial pressure index)
Elastin	The main component of elastic tissue. Elastic fibres are found in the extracellular matrix of skin, blood vessels and lungs, giving them the ability to recoil after transient stretch
Endothelium	The cells lining blood vessels
Endotoxin(s)	Produced mainly by Gram-negative organisms, for example *E. coli, Pseudomonas aeruginosa* and salmonella. These toxins do not diffuse into the interstitial fluid but are liberated when the cell eventually dies
Epithelium	Or epithelial tissue is the tissue that covers the body surface, lines body cavities and forms glands
Epithelialisation	The final stage of the proliferative phase
Erythema	A redness of the skin owing to hyperaemia
Eschar	A scab consisting of dried serum and devitalised dermal cells

Exotoxin(s)	Produced mainly by Gram-positive organisms, for example, *Clostridium tetani, Streptococcus pyogenes, Staphylococcus aureus*. These toxins diffuse easily into the interstitial fluid and are highly toxic
Extracellular matrix	Consists of ground substance and fibres. The ground substance is an amorphous gel-like material that fills the space between the cells and contains interstitial fluid and proteoglycans. The fibres consist of collagen, elastin and reticular fibres, the amounts and proportions of which vary depending on the type of tissue being scrutinised
Fibroblast	The cells that form fibrous tissue
Gram staining	A staining technique which allows for the differentiation of bacteria into Gram positive and Gram negative
Granulation	The formation of new tissue filling the defect which takes place during the proliferative phase of healing. The name is derived from the fact that the buds of new tissue take on the appearance of small granules
Growth factors	Peptides which are a sub-set of cytokines vital for cell proliferation
Healing by first intention	Also called primary intention. Wounds in this category are closed, thus leaving a minimal defect
Healing by second intention	Occurs when a wound is left open and allowed to heal by granulation
Healing by third intention	Sometimes called tertiary intention or delayed closure. Here the wound is left open often to assist drainage and is then closed surgically at a later date
Histamine	A protein that causes local dilation of blood vessels. The subsequent increased permeability allows leakage of fluid into the tissues and swelling results
Hypergranulation	Granulation tissue that is raised above the periwound area
Hypertrophic granulation	Develops soon after injury as a result of wounding from any cause, for example, vaccination, acne or surgery. More common in larger scars, burns. Unlike keloids these scars do not invade the skin beyond the wound margin
Infection	Micro-organisms are not only present but are multiplying and producing an associated host reaction. This reaction may take various forms and identification of infection can prove difficult for the novice. See also contamination and colonisation
Interleukins	Literally, between leucocytes; thse are growth factors that accumulate in areas where T-cells have been activated

Keloid	A thick protuberance of scar tissue. These outgrowths of excessive collagen continue to grow for some considerable time (years) and can invade the healthy periwound skin. Do not confuse with hypergranulation or hypertrophic scar
Lipodermatosclerosis	A brown staining of the lower limb as a result of the breakdown of haemoglobin. It is closely associated with venous hypertension and leg ulceration
Maceration	A softening or sogginess of the tissue owing to retention of excessive moisture
Necrosis	The local death of tissue. This tissue is often black/brown in colour and leathery in texture
Phagocytosis	The process of engulfing foreign matter by macrophages or neutrophils
Slough	Devitalised tissue which has a yellow/white/grey hue
Vasculitis	Inflammation of small arteries or veins with resulting fibrosis and thrombi formation. It is usually associated with rheumatoid disease

—

Index